9op

DIE ZAUBERFLÖTE

and

DIE ENTFÜHRUNG AUS DEM SERAIL

CASSELL OPERA GUIDES

W. A. MOZART

Die Zauberflöte

*

Die Entführung aus
dem Serail

Introduction by Brigid Brophy

CASSELL · LONDON

CASSELL & COMPANY LTD
35 Red Lion Square, London WC1
and at
SYDNEY · AUCKLAND
JOHANNESBURG · TORONTO

Devised and produced by
NORTON BAILEY LTD
103 Lonsdale Road, London SW13

First published 1971
Introduction © Brigid Brophy 1971
ISBN 0 304 93825 4

Printed in Great Britain by
Redwood Press Limited, Trowbridge & London

CONTENTS

DIE ZAUBERFLÖTE

Introduction

'Forgive me – I cannot help –
weeping – at the name of my Mozart'
　　　　　　Joseph Haydn (in 1807)[1]

The Key

Mozart was writing his father one of his usual lively letters of musical shop-talk when word reached him that his father was gravely ill. Giving his letter a fresh turn, Mozart said that, though he longed for better news, he had trained himself to be prepared for worse: he had 'formed such close relations' with death that its image no longer terrified but consoled him. 'And I thank my God', he continued, 'for graciously granting me the opportunity (you know what I mean) of learning that death is the *key* which unlocks the door to our true happiness. I never lie down at night without reflecting that – young as I am – I may not live to see another day. Yet no one of all my acquaintances could say that in company I am morose or disgruntled'.

That letter[2], the last surviving from Mozart to his father (who died in the following month, May 1787), is itself a key. It unlocks the opera which Mozart began composing four years after his father's death and finished only nine weeks before his own.

When, Where, for Whom

Die Zauberflöte is an opera which none of its acquaintances could

7

call morose or disgruntled. All Mozart's operas are deeply dramatic. (He intensively studied how to make them so[3].) *Die Zauberflöte* is also highly theatrical.

Mozart's was not a Wagnerian genius for imposing his will from above on everything down to the very design of the opera house but a classical and economic genius for exploiting the given, whether the available singers and instrumentalists or the existing styles and conventions. Mozart slipped into his opportunities, and shaped perfect and individualised artistic forms from inside.

Even while he was working, in Vienna, on *Die Zauberflöte*, he took another commission and a very different opportunity. He set off for Prague, began composing during the coach journey and in less than two months finished and launched *La clemenza di Tito*, an *opera seria* on a theme from classical history, in heroic Italian, with sung recitative linking the musical numbers[4]. *Tito* is a still under-appreciated psychological music-drama in the style of an operatic Racine (to whose *Bérénice* the plot of *Tito* is a sequel). On 30 September 1791, *Tito* was having the last night of its run in Prague, while in Vienna, at the Theater auf der Wieden[5], Mozart was conducting (from the pianoforte) the first performance of *Die Zauberflöte*, an opera in German whose linking dialogue is spoken and whose manner is pop.

The opportunity out of which Mozart created his pop opera was the theatrical flair of Emanuel Schikaneder, an actor-manager whom the Mozarts had known for just over a decade. To a play produced by Schikaneder Mozart had contributed an incidental aria; Schikaneder's company had mounted productions of Mozart's *Entführung* — as well as doing a *Hamlet* in Salzburg while Mozart was based there; after Mozart's move to Vienna* Schikaneder turned up *there*[6], became director of the Freihaus theatre in the suburb of Wieden and, in the spring of 1791, commissioned an opera from Mozart.

This wasn't (as *Die Entführung* itself bears splendid witness) Mozart's first opera to a text in his native language and with spoken dialogue. But Schikaneder's was one of the few commissions Mozart ever received, for work of any kind, from an impresario who himself depended directly on the public. Mozart's previous German operas were to private or imperial commissions — with the exception of *Zaide*, which he left unfinished precisely because it was an attempt on his part to go free-lance and the plans of the company he was composing it for went awry.

* see below

Not that official commissions hampered Mozart — whose practice, it is clear from every documented instance[8], was to wring exactly what he wanted from his librettists and whose genius was for expression through form. Joseph II found that *Die Entführung* contained 'very many notes, my dear Mozart', but neither his patronage nor his patronising prevented Mozart from giving the opera exactly (as he replied to the Emperor) the number of notes it needs. *Die Entführung* is taut, symmetrical and stylistically all-of-a-piece: in every good sense, formal. Yet its emotional subject-matter, the testing of love against the fear of death, is identical with that of *Die Zauberflöte*, where Mozart was externally much freer and whose music is strung so much more loosely and versatilely on the spoken dialogue.

Mozart needed no Schikaneder to free him to express himself. He had been doing that all along: in masterpieces. Schikaneder did, however, give him the opportunity to devise and freely elaborate his own *idiom* of theatrical expression.

In *Die Zauberflöte* Mozart was free to do anything he liked that could hold an audience. He could open with a dynamic, musically-continuous scene that is quite in the Italian grand-operatic manner (and is, indeed, structurally very like his own opening of *Don Giovanni*, with the same brilliant stroke of insinuating the hero into the audience's sympathy by introducing him on the run) and could follow it with the proletarian song of a bird-catcher, which sounds like a folk-tune (though Papageno's other, equally folkish song, 'Ein Mädchen', is in spirit and rhythm cousin to the quasi-hunting aria in high Italian which Handel allotted to a far classier huntsman-lover, Julius Caesar[9])

It is Mozart's imagination which holds *Die Zauberflöte* in unity. In doing so, his imagination has invented a new operatic genre (since attempted only, perhaps, by Richard Strauss and Hugo von Hofmannsthal in *Die Frau ohne Schatten*). Mozart is so masterly a theatrical expressionist that his enchanted episodes pass before the audience like an experience of surrealism, their logic as irrefutable as a dream's.

To Whose Text

The original printed libretto of *Die Zauberflöte* (which, by the eighteenth-century custom that ought never to have lapsed, was on sale at the theatre[10]) names Schikaneder as its author. In the 1840's, other claims to the authorship were advanced, at second hand, for other members of Schikaneder's company, including J.A. Haselbeck, prompter or theatre poet, who was said to have versified Schikaneder's prose sketches for the libretto, and J.G.K. Metzler who, under the pseudonym Gieseke, played the First Slave in the first production — before taking baroquely off on a second career, in which he lived Eskimo-fashion in Greenland and became professor of mineralogy at Trinity College, Dublin[11].

Scholarship debates the claims, but the likeliest explanation, to my mind, is that they are all true. The libretto reads like, precisely, a collaboration, a communal improvisation in a group of professional theatre people. Schikaneder, as the employer of all the others, would naturally have the final editorial power and, like a chairman, would put his name to the result.

Mozart himself, who worked on the music in a garden hut in the courtyard of the theatre and in a nearby lodgings of another member of the company (F.X. Gerl, the Sarastro)[12], should probably be counted among the librettists. If he followed his own precedents[8], he certainly influenced the dramatic line; and he was quite capable of contributing verbal lines. Indeed, some of the text is in doggerel of just the type which Mozart tossed into his letters.

> Mann und Weib, und Weib und Mann
> Reichen an die Gottheit an,

sing Pamina and Papageno. In a letter to his father[13], the newly-married Mozart had appended to his signature:

> Mann und Weib
> ist ein leib.

Pop — and Papa

Pop in diction, pop in structure (almost as much a continuous and cumulative revue as a dramatic development), *Die Zauberflöte* also exploits the audience-appeal of spectacle — so thoroughly, indeed, that one of the reasons given, some six months after the first performance, for not mounting a production in Berlin was that the 'beautiful and various sets and transformation effects', which 'crowd together every conceivable difficulty for the stage designer and machinists', couldn't be undertaken in a small theatre[14].

Against this grandeur of scenic design the opera sets an element of earthiness: Papageno. Even the claimant for Gieseke's authorship of the libretto attributed to Gieseke the statement that Papageno and Papagena were Schikaneder's invention. Certainly it was Schikaneder who, in the theatrical sense, 'created' the rôle of Papageno and whose professionalism sustained it. On 8 October 1791 Mozart himself, from the wings, played the glockenspiel that supplies the music Papageno ostensibly strikes from the bells. Mozart played an arpeggio at a moment when Schikaneder was not 'playing' (the first intimation most of the audience had, says Mozart's account to his wife[15], that the actor didn't provide his own music). Schikaneder kept his theatrical head. When Mozart played a chord into another pause, Schikaneder 'struck the glockenspiel and said *"Shut up"*. Whereupon everyone laughed',

Papageno's suicide attempt is as old as the *commedia dell'arte*. (Jean-Louis Barrault mimes such an attempt in *Les Enfants du Paradis*). His engagement to what seems to be a crone, who by happy magic turns out to be a girl, is as old as Chaucer. (The joke of Papageno's astonishment when he asks the crone her age and is told 'eighteen years and two minutes' is perhaps Mozart's own; for in another of his newly-married letters[16], when his wife was 20, Mozart remarks, in a post-script, to his father: 'my wife is almost ninety-one'). Papageno's boasting is from Plautus and his pipes from Pan.

It is directly from the *commedia dell'arte* that Papageno gets his tendency to answer the question 'Who are you?' with 'A man'- together, perhaps, with the rudiments of his nature, since there seems to have been a tradition going back to late Rome for clowns to strut and blow through a whistle, in imitation of birds[17]. But it is probably through an original poeticism (though inspired, perhaps, by the ambiguous species of Caliban[18]) that Papageno is simultaneously a birdcatcher and (presumably in order to decoy his victims) virtually a bird himself.('From your feathers', Tamino says to him at their first meeting, 'I'd take you for -' 'Not for a bird?' interrupts Papageno.) Schikaneder, a Hamlet turned clown, played him not as a hobbledehoy but, as an illustration in the original libretto shews, as a spruce and upstanding man-bird.

Papageno, whose Italianate name is traditionally pronounced in the German way, with the *g* hard, is, I think, a pun both Italian and German. His name (modelled on *pappagallo, parrot* – with a touch, in keeping with his character, of *pappare, to gobble*) falls apart into the elements *Papa* and *gen* (as in *philoprogenitive*). Papageno's ambition is to become a papa: of 'first a little Papageno, then a little Papagena'. In furtherance of his ambition he wishes he could catch girls as well as birds. Indeed, his very profession ('Der Vogelfänger bin ich ja') puns on his behalf. As Freud's translator[19] footnotes Freud's account of the erotic significance of dreams of flying, it is a 'reference to the German slang word *"vögeln"* (to copulate) from *"Vogel"* (a bird)'.

In his capacity of musical bird, Papageno probably held a personal significance for Mozart (or perhaps Mozart was one of his inventors). In 1784 Mozart bought a starling who could whistle a version of a tune he had recently composed. Three years later, when the starling died, Mozart wrote, very much in the eighteenth-century manner (of, for instance, Thomas Gray's *On the Death of a Favourite Cat, Drowned in a Tub of Gold Fishes*), an elegiac poem. More idiosyncratically, he insisted on holding a funeral procession and a requiem[20] — a strange psychological gesture that I can interpret only as a symptom of Mozart's ambivalent and overwhelming reaction to his father's death. Mozart's father had died six days before the starling.

That requiem for another bird, a requiem which in psychological essence was probably for his own papa, must have been brought back to Mozart's mind, during the composition of his opera about Papageno, by the mysteriously anonymous commission he received for a requiem mass — a work which he declared, as he composed it, to be his own requiem[21] and which indeed he did not live to finish.

In the last year of his life Mozart kept a canary —which (his sister-in-law afterwards remembered) had to be removed from the next room when Mozart was dying because its singing 'overtaxed his emotions'. What it sang was, I suspect, a tune or tunes from *Die Zauberflöte*. During much of the composition and rehearsal (and indeed during the opening) of the opera, Mozart's wife was taking the cure at Baden. In June Mozart and some friends ('three carriage-fuls of us') made an excursion, in the course of which he hoped to visit his wife. Writing[22] to her about the plan, Mozart said: 'It is only a pity that I can't take with me either the clavier or the bird!' On the clavier, obviously, he would have played her some of the opera he was composing: the bird, perhaps would have whistled her some.

The Sources

Part of *Die Zauberflöte's* originality lies in its original mixture of established categories. It is set, like a regular *opera seria,* in the ancient world, where the mystery cult of Isis and Osiris is still extant. Inasmuch as information about that cult came chiefly from Greco-Roman writers like Apuleius and Diodorus Siculus, *Die Zauberflöte* is a classical opera. But since the Greco-Roman cult originated in Egypt, the opera has already picked itself an exotic corner of the ancient world: and this it enlarges by making Tamino a Japanese, who has strayed into territory so alien to him that he questions everyone he meets about its institutions. Thus *Die Zauberflöte* is also an exotic opera, in the same large eighteenth-century category as *Die Entführung* and the fictitious travellers' tales of Voltaire, Montesquieu and Horace Walpole.

However, Tamino is, as well as exotic, a prince — and one who seeks wisdom by way of initiation into the cult. That is the opera's entrée to a third favourite group, stories (like Dr. Johnson's *Rasselas*) about the education of princes — a matter of urgent concern to eighteenth-century Europe which, if it couldn't rid itself of its hereditary rulers, hoped that the *philosophes*, the Encyclopaedists and the whole movement of thought called the Enlightenment would, at least, educate them.

This mixture of categories the opera borrowed from its main source-book, *The Life of Sethos*, a novel by Jean Terrasson which was published anonymously in Paris in 1731 and promptly translated into English and into German[23] (whence its hero's name was borrowed by a German play[24] for which Mozart composed incidental music). Terrasson's story, set in the ancient world, purports to be told by a Greek and concerns the education of Prince Sethos (into a constitutional, rational and tolerant ruler) by his initiation into a rationalised version of the Egyptian cult of Isis. In the underground temple of the priests, Sethos, warned by an inscription that there is no turning back (a warning which, in places almost word for word, is in the opera delivered by the Two Armed Men), goes through an obstacle-race of ordeals comparable, though not identical, to the ordeals in the opera[25].

Into Terrasson's mixture the opera introduces another theme: magic. C.M. Wieland (whom Mozart had met in Mannheim in 1777) made, under the title *Dschinnistan* (whose final volume appeared in

13

1789), a collection of exotic magical stories which provided operatic themes alike for Schikaneder and for a rival impresario. Mozart's opera of 1791 took its title from a story by A.J. Liebeskind, collected by Wieland: *Lulu, oder die Zauberflöte*. Magic is not so incompatible as it looks with Terrasson's rational antiquarianism. The magic opera *Oberon*, which Schikaneder put on in May 1791, its rival, which appeared in June, *[Kaspar] Der Fagottist, oder die Zauberzither (Kaspar the Bassoonist, or The Magic Zither)*, and *Die Zauberflöte* itself, which appeared in September, are all from stories in Wieland's collection, and are all concerned with magic musical instruments (Oberon's being a horn)[26]. As librettos they are (another category that can claim *Die Zauberflöte*) literary tributes to the magic of music, like Dryden's *Alexander's Feast* (Handel's setting of which Mozart had re-orchestrated the year before). The standard classical image for such compliments was Orpheus: and *Sethos* includes a detour that re-tells the Orpheus story. (With his passion for rationalising, Terrasson makes out that the myth of Orpheus's visit to the underworld is a disguised account of Orpheus's initiation in the underground temple). I think it is plainly Orpheus whom the opera has in mind when Tamino's flute enchants the animals.

If that theme, like most of the opera's themes, was from *Sethos*, it was, I suspect, shaped by Mozart himself—out of his personal liking for animals plus the memory (brought back to Mozart's intensely verbal mind by the title and theme of *Die Zauberflöte*) of a poem which, employing the standard complimentary image, a friend had in 1787 written by way of tribute in Mozart's album: 'When Orpheus's magic lute *(Zauberlaute)* plays, Amphion sings to the lyre, Then the lion goes tame, the rivers stand still, The tiger eavesdrops, and rocks move'[27].

The Code

The other reason (besides its scenic complexity) given for not immediately putting on *Die Zauberflöte* in Berlin was that it could not interest .an audience 'which is ignorant of certain mysteries'. Mozart and Schikaneder (and, incidentally, Gieseke) were Freemasons. Even to outsiders it was clear that the opera was a secret allegory. To Masons the printed libretto cryptically advertised itself as such: one of its illustrations, which shews a temple, is littered with Masonic symbols[28].

The mode of Masonic ceremonies is, in the words of one of them, 'the Catechetical, or, in more familiar terms, by question and answer' – a mode the opera uses in the dialogue between Tamino and the Speaker. To 'What is Freemasonry?', Freemasonry catechetically replies 'A peculiar system of Morality, veiled in Allegory, and illustrated by Symbols': a just description of *Die Zauberflöte*.

Masonry is veiled not only in allegory but in secrecy and hierarchy. At each of its three grades of initiation, the initiate is informed of symbols (and their moralistic meaning) which he swears on pain of death not to divulge. The elaboration of the symbolism (which in reality has been repeatedly divulged[29]) enables initiates to refer to the secrets in code, in a manner that makes sense to fellow-initiates but gives nothing away to outsiders. This game, which the opera plays extensively, Masonry inherited or copied from the ancient-world mysteries which in the opera stand for Masonry. In the second century Apuleius was initiated, like Tamino after him, into the cult of Isis, and he ends his account of his initiation with the words. 'There, I've told you things which even though you've heard them you of necessity still don't know'[30].

Masonry's central allegory, the triumph of light over dark, is shared with the very metaphor of the Enlightenment, with everyday speech (which says 'I see' in the sense of 'I understand') and with the cult of Osiris (the sun) and Isis (the moon, which can illuminate even the night). In pursuit of the allegory, a first-degree initiant into Masonry is blindfolded and presented as 'a poor Candidate in a state of darkness' (with, incidentally, one foot slipshod – in token of which Tamino, when he is led in to receive the warning of the Armed Men, is, according to the stage directions, 'without sandals'). The candidates in the opera undergo the Masonic darkness by being, at various times, veiled, subjected to ordeal-by-darkness and aware of spiritual darkness (Tamino's 'everlasting night'); their spiritual enlightenment at initiation coincides with Sarastro's victory, in which 'the sun's rays expel night'.

Masonry submits its candidates to a test (by catechism) and to a peril. At the first degree, the candidate has (though, being blindfolded, he can't see it) a dagger presented to his breast; at the final degree he is symbolically murdered and resurrected. Initiation consists of overcoming the fear of death. It is in that sense that Tamino represents Orpheus, who descended into the realm of the dead.

The Masonic 'test of merit' Mozart represents, I think, in the overture — by a witty personal allusion; for the Allegro theme (beginning at bar 16) is, as contemporaries noticed, from a sonata by M. Clementi, and it is the very sonata which Clementi played when, in 1781, Joseph II indeed tested Mozart's merit by holding a piano contest between Mozart and Clementi[31]. The Masonic perils the opera represents, in general, by the ordeals. In particular, the Masonic dagger appears, I suspect, as the dagger the Queen gives Pamina. It is when Pamina has proved, by turning the dagger on herself, that she 'has no fear of night and death' that she is pronounced 'worthy' of initiation. For although the opera reflects the anti-feminism of Masonry in the Speaker's generalisations, Sarastro's paternalism and the pain (which she so rendingly expressed in 'Ach, ich fühl's') imposed on Pamina by Tamino's ordeal-by-silence, the drama at its climax gives the lie to its own text. Sarastro's sanctimonious axiom that Pamina needs a man to guide her is overturned when, at their shared ordeals, Pamina magnificently tells Tamino that *she* will lead *him*[32].

Masonic virtues, ornaments and tools (the craft-tools of building, which, since Masons 'are not all operative', are endowed also with moralistic meanings) go in threes. Hence the opera's Three Ladies, Three Boys or Genii (who are not listed in the cast of the first production, so perhaps the Ladies doubled their parts), and three Temples (which I take to be the 'three great pillars', representing Wisdom, Strength and Beauty, of a Masonic Lodge). Hence also the three commands of the Three Boys: Tamino is to be 'constant, patient and secret', just as the newly initiated Mason is charged with 'Secrecy, Fidelity and Obedience'. A Masonic candidature is announced by three knocks: hence Tamino's knocking at three Temple-doors. However, the Masonic knocks were sometimes elaborated[33] into a code more intricate than morse. The opera is probably giving highly specific information through the various rhythms enunciated by the chords which, in groups of three, open and punctuate the overture and by the threefold woodwind-and-brass calls which precede the dialogue where Sarastro, representing the Master of a Lodge, catechises the priests about the candidate's qualifications.

Neither do I doubt there is, though abstrusely, Masonic meaning in the gift to Tamino and Papageno of three talismans: magic flute, magic bells and a portrait Tamino calls 'magickedly beautiful'. 'Magic' probably stands for 'Masonic'. By borrowing a story-title about a flute, the opera defies Mozart's dislike[34] of the instrument.

(He composed for it, but to commission). Part of the flute's value to the creators of the opera was, I think, that it fitted available accomplishments. Benedikt Schack, who sang Tamino, was a flautist[35] — which must have enabled him, at the least, to *look* as plausible in his 'playing' as Schikaneder in *his*. But I suspect that the flute was not merely convenient but indispensable: because it is, uniquely (apart from its piccolo version) a transverse instrument. When Tamino plays his flute and enters the final ordeals, his head and the flute sketch a right-angle. Masonic initiants arrange their feet in that shape — in token of the mason's square, which is one of the three 'movable jewels' of a Lodge (and one of the three tools of the second degree) and on which Masonry places the moralistic value which has entered English idiom in the Masonic phrase 'on the square'.

The Plot Change Hypothesis

The claim that Haselbeck was the versifier of the libretto was made in 1840 by Ignaz von Seyfried, who had joined Schikaneder's company eight years after *Die Zauberflöte* appeared. Writing at the age of 64 or so, Seyfried continued with an account of how, when Seyfried was about 15, the libretto was formed: it was 'complete as far as the first finale' when Schikaneder's rival put on *his* magic opera (which, though its title has transformed a flute into a bassoon and a zither, is based on the story from which *Die Zauberflöte* takes its title). Schikaneder, Seyfried said, responded by altering 'the entire plan' of *Die Zauberflöte* and thereby 'saved and made the fortune of the whole'[36].

The reason Seyfried gives (and was perhaps given) for the change seems thin, since the eighteenth century was not much worried about plagiarism and the supposedly rival opera, though it appeared first, had obligingly not used the title of the story. Mozart went to see *Der Fagottist* on 11 June, judged it 'shoddy stuff' and shewed, in reporting to his wife[37], no anxiety. All the same, the notion that the plot of *Die Zauberflöte* did suffer a change of direction seems, to most Mozartians (except Alfred Einstein), supported by the internal evidence of the opera itself — though I guess that the true reason for the change, which would naturally not be told to a boy of 15, concerned Masonry. Perhaps the opera was shewing the secrets too transparently.

According to Seyfried, it was part of the *text* that was already finished when the change was made — in which case the authors were reckless if they didn't go back and alter the earlier part into consistency with the new plan. Seyfried's account makes sense, however, if some of the *music* was already composed. The words which had already been set to music couldn't be changed. They would have to be incorporated, as Seyfried implies, into the 'whole' which was thereby 'saved' – with the result that the change of direction is still detectable in the opera.

Even if *Der Fagottist* wasn't the true occasion of the change, its appearance, since the explanation was plausible to Seyfried, must mark roughly the date of the change. And Mozart did indeed compose some of *Die Zauberflöte* before he saw (which he did only three days after its opening) *Der Fagottist.* On the morning of his visit to the theatre, 'out of sheer boredom' he 'composed an aria for' his own opera[38].

Seyfried is convincing if his 'complete as far as the first finale' means that the music was complete up to the point where the Act I finale is due to begin[39] (which it does with the Three Boys leading Tamino towards the Temples). It is precisely *during* that finale that the opera changes direction – when the Speaker conveys to Tamino that the Queen, whom Tamino and the audience have so far taken to be a goody, is a baddy (which, for the rest of the opera, she is). The signs are strong that up to that point the authors intended the Queen to be a genuinely good power. Her Ladies practise exactly the Masonic morality which the opera finally endorses; the Masonic Genii emanate from her; it is she who sends Tamino the flute by whose virtue he wins initiation. Authors may have to make nonsense of their own schemes, but it would be a nonsensical allegory indeed which from the start *intended* Tamino to be initiated by courtesy of an enemy of Masonry.

The hypothesis is clinched, I think, by the Masonic symbolism. In the light versus darkness allegory, the power of darkness resides in Monostatos, whose 'soul is as black as' his face. The title of the Queen of the Night, on the other hand, need not imply that the Queen herself is a dark power. Indeed, to Masons it would imply the opposite. The Queen of the Night is the Queen who rules *over* and illuminates the night. She is in fact the second of Masonry's 'three lesser lights', which are 'the Sun to rule the day, the Moon to govern the night, and the Worshipful Master to rule and direct the Lodge'.

That the Queen was designed as a figure of illumination is confirmed by her other name, the 'star-blazing' (*sternflammende*) Queen. That title, I surmise, Masons could not have given to a figure they meant to be evil. The Blazing Star is the second of the three 'ornaments' of a Masonic Lodge. Indeed there was a German Lodge, roughly contemporary with *Die Zauberflöte*, named the Blazing Star (*Zum flammenden Stern)*[40].

As the moon, the Queen (as her airborne irruptions into the opera bear out) is a figure of Isis. Obviously she was originally intended to be on the same side as the cult of Isis (though perhaps a reconciliation between her and Sarastro, as between fellow members of a Lodge, was due to be worked out by the drama). The Queen is star-blazing because she is surrounded by stars (her Ladies). And indeed the heraldic diagram which Masonry calls the 'First Tracing Board' is dominated by a sun in glory (the rays which triumph at the end of the opera) and, surrounded by seven (for the seven officers of a Lodge) stars, a moon.

The Significance

Mozart's last letter to his father, with its complicit and encoded 'you know what I mean', is from a Mason to a Mason. Masonry was deep-involved in the crucial relationship of Mozart's life[41], his relation to his father.

Leopold Mozart was multiply and uniquely an authority to his son: not only father but tutor, agent, manager and editor throughout that miracle-working childhood and beyond. And it was on the question of authority, this time on the socio-political scale, that Mozart came into variance with the authority of his father. Leopold Mozart stayed conservatively in the feudalism of Salzburg, fearful and disapproving when Mozart, resenting that insolence of princes which treated him as a servant and placed him at table below the valets (though above, he noted, the cooks)[42], set up independently in Vienna and, again without his father's authorisation, married.

Although Mozart was still a Catholic on his deathbed, which was attended (unwillingly) by a priest, he also became (in December 1784) a Mason. (Masonry was ambiguously treated by Catholic rulers and explicitly condemned by papal bulls). Yet four months later, Leopold Mozart, for all his conservatism, joined the same Lodge[43]. The son had led the father into initiation, as Pamina leads Tamino.

To Mozart, who in the following year chose to make his new opera from Beaumarchais's revolutionary *Figaro* (a play Leopold Mozart found 'tiresome')[44], one of the virtues of Masonry was its egalitarianism. That quality may seem contradicted by the hierarchical structure. But Masonry, with its allegory of illumination and its description of itself as 'a progressive science', is a metaphor of education. Indeed, the moralistic meaning of the Masonic chisel is 'the advantages of education, by which means we are rendered fit members of regularly organised society'. Within its own limited society Masonry, with its grades of initiation, acted out the great eighteenth-century wish for society at large, that the people with the most power should be the best educated.

Masons meet each other not only 'on the square' but 'on the level' (in the brotherly spirit commended by Sarastro): a reference to the builder's level (another of the Masonic tools), whose 'operative' purpose is 'to say levels' and whose moral one is to teach 'equality' and that 'we have all sprung from the same stock'. I think it likely that in *Die Zauberflöte* the Masonic level is represented by Pamina's portrait. A portrait is a likeness. It is like, level with and equivalent to (ideas which in German are all embodied in the same adjective, *gleich*) the person who sat for it. That is the point Papageno proves when he compares the portrait, item by item, with Pamina in the flesh. Instantly, the opera dramatises the Masonic moral: the quasi-love duet, the opera's great statement of the equality between man and wife and their united supremacy, is sung not by the lovers, a prince and princess, but by the princess and her mother's servant.

The world, however, didn't follow the Masonic model. Haydn, whose response to Mozart is one of the most movingly generous in the history of art (and whom Mozart, significantly, called his papa[45]), was indignant[46] that the world didn't provide a living for the man he called 'the greatest composer known to me either in person or by name'[47]. The letters of Mozart's last four years chronicle an agony: desperate, ashamed borrowings from fellow-Masons; desperate promises to his wife that they would manage, that he would take pupils, that he would, above all, *work*[48]. (Tamino learns from the inscriptions on the Temples that they are the seat of Wisdom, Art and *Work*.) Mozart had been famous since his early childhood. Partly because there was no royalty system for paying composers of opera after the outright fee for the first production, but partly also because of the world's philistinism that still oppresses creative artists, his fame prompted the world to ask him for more work, but not to appreciate or pay him a living wage for what he had already done.

His famous childhood was a working childhood, and it destroyed his health. By the time Mozart was 31, his doctor had twice saved him from death[49]. Mozart valued Masonry not only for its hope of egalitarianism in working life but for its promise of overcoming the fear of death. Invoking Masonry to reconcile him to the prospect of his father's death, Mozart was already, in his last letter to his father, confronting his own. His constant reflexion, 'young as I am − I may not live to see another day', is the sense of mortality that gives immortality to all his music and, most particularly, to the music of *Die Zauberflöte*, his opera about a triumph over the fear of death. While he was composing it, he wrote to his wife[50]: 'If I go to the piano and sing something out of my opera, I have to stop at once, for this stirs my emotions too deeply'.

(And perhaps the reason why his emotions were stirred too deeply, as he lay mortally ill, by the canary in the next room was that the canary, too, was singing something out of his opera − an reminding him of his other pet bird, whose death he had mentally amalgamated with his father's.)

Young as he still was (35), during the night of 5−6 December 1791, after trying to explain how he wanted his requiem completed and after believing in delirium that he was at the theatre listening to *Die Zauberflöte*[51], Mozart died: of miliary fever, according to the registration of the death; of uraemia, according to modern diagnosis; of poison, according to Salieri's babblings in madness[52] (a confession, surely, not of the deed but of the envious wish): and ultimately, as was clear to his contemporaries, including his widow[53], of 'over-exertion'. He was buried in the cheapest type of grave, a communal one[54], and nobody bothered to mark its whereabouts. In 1799 Wieland, distantly one of the ancestors of *Die Zauberflöte*, wrote[55] 'Good Mozart! you erected a gravestone to a favourite bird in a garden which you rented, and you even wrote an epitaph for him. When will that be done for you which you did for your bird?'

[1] Haydn's 1807 utterance was reported in 1808. O.E. Deutsch: *Mozart A Documentary Biography* (Black, 1965), p.503. [2] 4 April 1787. I have quoted Emily Anderson's translation (Macmillan, 1966) of this and other letters of the Mozarts. [3] One of dozens of instances: J. Frank recorded in detail Mozart's study of operatic scores for their 'dramatic effectiveness' (O.E. Deutsch, p.561). [4] Mozart's composing in the coach was recorded by F.X. Niemetschek (Prague 1808), who held that those of the *Tito* recitatives which are not orchestrally accompanied are by a pupil (later conjectured to be F.X. Süssmayr). That this need not be so I have argued in an article 'Pro *Tito*' (*Musical Times*, June 1969). [5] Mozart remarked the last and first nights' coincidence in his letter of 7–8 October 1791. The playbill for *Die Zauberflöte* is reproduced in *Mozart und seine Welt* (Bärenreiter Kassel, 1961), p.257. [6] Mozart's now lost aria of 1780 for Schikaneder is discussed in letters between Mozart and his father (E. Anderson, pp. 660–79). *Entführung* productions are recorded in O.E. Deutsch, p.229, p.291. Mozart discussed the dramatic effectiveness of the ghost in *Hamlet* by letter in November 1780; Schikaneder had produced *Hamlet* in Salzburg the previous month; Mozart, as his widow reported, read Shakespeare in translation (E. Anderson, p.674; O.E. Deutsch, p.539). Schikaneder settled in Vienna and took the directorship of the Freihaus theatre 'auf der Wieden' in 1789 (A. Einstein: Mozart, Cassell 1956, p.461). Einstein (p.462) dates the *Zauberflöte* commission to 'spring', Paul Nettl, in *Mozart and Masonry* (Philosophical Library, N.Y., 1957), p.67, to 'March 7, 1791'.

[7] The 'very many notes' exchange was reported by Niemetschek. *Zaide* is the title posthumously given to K.344 (A. Einstein, pp.452–3). [8] Mozart's letters of November 1780 document the libretto changes he required for *Idomeneo*. For an *Entführung* aria, he 'explained' the words he wanted to his librettist (Mozart to his father, 26 September 1781). For *Figaro* Mozart's father (letter of 11 November 1785) predicted much discussion before Mozart 'gets the libretto so adjusted as to suit his purpose exactly'. In his own catalogue Mozart entered *Tito* (a libretto originally in three acts, by Metastasio) as an *opera seria* in two acts 'reduced', by C. Mazzola, 'to a real opera'. [9] 'Va tacito e nascosto', Giulio Cesare, 1724. Mozart re-orchestrated four of Handel's English vocal works for performance

in Vienna between 1788 and 1790, and his widow attested Mozart's informed admiration for Handel (O.E. Deutsch, p.541). [10] — as the playbill states. Mozart's letter of 8—9 October 1791 relates that Mozart intended to take his mother-in-law to *Die Zauberflöte* and that she was given the libretto to read beforehand. [11] The claim for Haselbeck (or Haselböck) was made in 1840 by I. von Seyfried; according to Deutsch, Haselbeck was not prompter but a theatre poet, which perhaps helps his claim (O.E. Deutsch, p.555). Gieseke's claim (O.E. Deutsch, p.560) was put forward in 1849 (when Gieseke was dead) by Julius Cornet, who contradicts another claim, said to have been widely believed, for yet another member of the company. Gieseke's career is described by P. Nettl (who spells him Giesecke), pp.63—64.

[12] O.E. Deutsch, pp.555—6. [13] 24 August 1782 (Mozart married on 4 August). [14] O.E. Deutsch, p.444. [15] Letter of 8—9 October 1791. [16] 11 September 1782. (Constanze was born on 5 January 1762; O.E. Deutsch, p.205).

[17] The exchange 'Who are you?' etc. is quoted from *commedia dell'arte* in Kay Dick: *Pierrot* (Hutchinson 1960), p.41 and bird-clowning mentioned on p.81. [18] Cf. note 6. Anne Righter's edition of *The Tempest* (Penguin 1968), p.19, says Mozart 'sketched out but did not live to write an opera based on' *The Tempest;* but she doesn't say, and I can't find, what the statement is based on. E.J. Dent (*Mozart's Operas,* Oxford, 1949, p.262) notes two operatic versions, by other composers, in 1798. [19] A.A. Brill (S. Freud: *The Interpretation of Dreams,* Allen & Unwin, 1945, p.371).

[20] O.E. Deutsch, p.225. Mozart entered in his expenses book, under 27 May 1784, the purchase of the starling and a version of the tune — which is the rondo theme from his piano concerto K.453, one of the concerti Mozart had sent to his father on 15 May (E. Anderson, p.513). Mozart's verses on the starling's death are published in Mozart: *Briefe und Aufzeichnungen* (Bärenreiter Kassel 1963, Vol. IV, pp.49—50. [21] O.E. Deutsch, p.439, p.511.

[22] 7 June 1791. The account of the canary given by Mozart's sister-in-law Sophie is in O.E. Deutsch, p.527. [23] The English translation of *Sethos* is dated 1732, which is also (P. Nettl, p.72) the date of the first German translation. According to P. Nettl, E. Duller recognised *Sethos* as a source of the opera in 1837. E.J. Dent (p.225) assigns the first recognition to Thomas Love

Peacock, in a review of 1827. [24] T.P. Gebler's *Thomas, König in Ägypten;* Mozart's incidental music was probably first performed in its entirety in 1779–80 (O.E. Deutsch, p.145). The name *Sethos* is used when the hero goes into disguise. [25] Brigid Brophy: *Mozart the Dramatist* (Faber 1964), pp.128–202. [26] Mozart's letter of 10 January 1778; O.E. Deutsch, p.397, p.556, p.560; P. Nettl, p.68.
[27] I have literally-translated the German text (by J. Hurdalek) which is published, under 12 November 1787, in the German edition (Bärenreiter Kassel, 1961) of O.E. Deutsch. [28] P. Nettl (p.82) interprets the five-pointed star as the symbol of the second degree and describes the instruments at the bottom right of the picture as symbols 'of the first degree, square and trowel, and an hour-glass representing the third'. The 'working tools' (but these may be different from 'symbols') of the first degree are usually given as gauge, gavel and chisel (*Text Book of Freemasonry*, p.34; James Dewar: *The Unlocked Secret,* Kimber 1966, p.144). The 'square' in the illustration to the libretto looks more like a pick: one side is curved, so it doesn't make a right-angle. The hourglass, being in two equal halves, might, I suppose, represent the Masonic compasses, which have two equal legs.
[29] My quotations are from an undated, probably early 20th century *Text Book,* but the same material is given by J. Dewar (see note 28).
[30] *Metamorphoses (The Golden Ass),* XI, 23. [31] O.E. Deutsch, p.198, pp.541–3. Emily Anderson queries the resemblance in her footnote to Mozart's account of the contest, which is in his letter of 16 January, 1782. [32] Michael Levey: 'Aspects of Mozart's Heroines' *Warburg Journal,* XXII, 1–2, 1959. [33] One such code, French, is set out in *Manuel Maçonnique . . .,* Paris, 1820.
[34] O.E. Deutsch, p.561. [35] E. Anderson, p.940; O.E. Deutsch, p.408. [36] O.E. Deutsch, pp.555–6. [37] Letter of 12 June 1791. [38] Letter of 11 June 1791. [39] Some scholars assume that the entire first act was finished before the change was made. One scholar even makes that assumption plus the assumption that it was only at the change that Masonry was introduced, though himself discerning Masonic significance in Tamino's 'everlasting night' cry of Act I. *Der Fagottist* appeared on 8th June. If this marks the date or approximate date of the change in *Die Zauberflöte,* it is quite plausible that Mozart had not by then finished the whole of Act I. He would still have had time to compose the Act I finale and fit in to the timetable implied by his letter of 2 July to his wife, where he sent a

message to Süssmayr asking him to send (send back, presumably) the score of Act I so that Mozart could orchestrate it. If, however, the outline of Act II was changed circa 8 June, the change cannot have amounted to a complete re-writing of the verbal expressions in the libretto. Mozart's letter of 11 June to his wife quotes 'Tod und Verzweiflung war sein Lohn', which is from the text (as it now stands) of the priests' duet early on in Act II. [40] P. Nettl, p.39. [41] B. Brophy, pp.230–65. [42] Mozart's letters of 12 May and 17 March 1781. [43] E. Anderson, p.976; O.E. Deutsch, p.230, p.241. Masonry was condemned by Papal Bulls of 1738 and 1751. [44] L. Da Ponte: *Memoirs* (1823–7), Routledge 1929, p.129; E. Anderson, p.893. [45] O.E. Deutsch, p.489. [46] O.E. Deutsch, p.308. [47] E. Anderson, p.886. [48] e.g. E. Anderson, p.942, p.945. [49] O.E. Deutsch, p.289. [50] 7 July 1791. [51] E. Anderson, pp.976–7; O.E. Deutsch, p.556. [52] O.E. Deutsch, pp.514–6, p.527. [53] O.E. Deutsch, p.527, p.540. [54] O.E. Deutsch, p.417. [55] O.E. Deutsch, p.489.

DIE ZAUBERFLÖTE

Libretto by Emanuel Schikaneder

DRAMATIS PERSONAE

SARASTRO
TAMINO
THE SPEAKER/OLD PRIEST
SECOND PRIEST
THE QUEEN OF THE NIGHT
PAMINA, *her daughter*
THREE LADIES *of the Queen of the Night*
THREE BOYS
PAPAGENO
PAPAGENA
MONOSTATOS, *a Moor*
TWO MEN IN ARMOUR
THREE SLAVES

CHORUS of Priests, attendants, people, slaves, etc.

Synopsis

ACT I

Mountainous landscape with a temple. Tamino, pursued by a huge serpent, falls unconscious. The three ladies of the Queen of the Night come out of the temple and slay the monster. Unable to decide which of them will stay to guard the handsome youth, they all three return to the temple. Papageno, a birdcatcher who lives by barter, comes to deliver his quota of birds to the Queen's ladies, and boasts to the recovered Tamino that it was he who slew the serpent. He is punished for lying by the ladies, who return with a padlock for his mouth and a miniature portrait for Tamino. It is of Pamina, the Queen's daughter, and he is bewitched by her beauty. They tell him how she was abducted by an evil magician, and he determines to rescue her. The mountains divide to reveal the Queen's throne room: she tells him that he is indeed the man destined to rescue Pamina and marry her as his reward. The palace vanishes. The three ladies release Papageno from his padlock, present Tamino with a magic flute to protect and sustain him, and persuade an unwilling Papageno to accompany Tamino by presenting him with a magic chime of bells. Three boys will guide them on their way to Sarastro's realm—for such is the magician's name.
A splendid Egyptian room. Following a vain attempt to escape Monostatos, Pamina has been recaptured and the Moor leads her in swooning. Papageno suddenly appears, and the outlandish appearance of each terrifies the other so much that both he and Monostatos retreat. Papageno returns and tells Pamina that her rescue by Prince Tamino is imminent.

A grove with three temples. The three boys lead Tamino on and then disappear. Unseen voices turn him away from the Temples of Reason and Nature, but when he knocks at the Temple of Wisdom the Speaker, an old priest, comes out, and in the course of a conversation tells Tamino that he has been deceived by the Queen, that Sarastro is ruler in the Temple of Wisdom and that all will be made clear when he enters the communion of the brotherhood. Unseen voices tell him that this will be soon, or never. Tamino plays the magic flute, and the animals come out of the woods to listen. His playing is answered by Papageno's pan pipes, and he hurries away to find the birdcatcher. Papageno and Pamina enter, hotly pursued by Monostatos and the slaves, whose attempts to capture them are foiled by the magic chimes. Sarastro and his entourage enter. Pamina confesses that her attempted escape was prompted by Monostatos's lust. Tamino is then led on by the triumphant Moor, but Sarastro orders him to be beaten and directs the priests to take Tamino and Papageno to the temple of ordeals.

ACT II

A palm grove. The priests discuss Tamino's case. Sarastro mentions that Pamina was destined by the gods for Tamino, and that this was the reason for her abduction. He orders the Speaker to conduct Tamino and Papageno through their trials and calls on Isis and Osiris for guidance.

A forecourt of the temple. The priests ask Tamino and Papageno if they are willing to undergo the ordeals—Papageno needs the promise of a wife before he agrees—and the first test is that of silence. The three ladies appear, try to turn them against the priests, and warn them that the Queen is in the temple precincts. A fearful thunderclap and a call from the priests cause the ladies to vanish.

A beautiful garden by moonlight. Pamina lies asleep. As Monostatos steals lustfully towards her, the Queen of the Night appears, and he withdraws. Pamina awakes, and her mother tells her that if she is to save Tamino from the priests and regain the shield of the sun given to the priests by her father (once Sarastro's associate), she must kill Sarastro, and the Queen gives her a dagger. Monostatos, who has overheard all this, tries to blackmail Pamina into loving him, and when he is dismissed with contempt by Sarastro himself, he slinks away to join forces with the Queen. Sarastro tells Pamina of the principles of love and mercy honoured by the brethren.

A hall. The priests once more bid the initiates keep silent. An ancient crone brings Papageno a glass of water, and claims to be his sweetheart. The three boys fly in with the magic flute and chimes, temporarily lost, and some food for Papageno. Pamina enters, and utterly bewildered by Tamino's silence is brought to the brink of despair.

A vault. Sarastro commends Tamino's conduct so far, and bids him take leave of Pamina before the final ordeals. Papageno, alone for the first time, sings of his longing for a woman to share his life. The crone enters and is momentarily transformed into his Papagena, but the Speaker intervenes, saying he is not yet worthy of her.

A garden. Pamina, brought to distraction by conflicting emotions and the continued absence of Tamino, contemplates suicide. She is prevented by the three boys, who promise to take her to Tamino.

Two great mountains, one containing a waterfall, the other spewing forth fire. Two armed men tell Tamino that to attain full enlightenment he must pass through fire, water, air and earth. He is about to enter the fire when Pamina's voice is heard without. She runs to join him in the last ordeals, and together, protected by the flute, they pass through the elements.

The garden, as above. Papageno, searching in vain fo. Papagena, determines to kill himself. The three boys suggest he plays his magic chimes instead, and when he does so they lead his wife to him. Papageno and Papagena propose to rear a large family.

A subterranean vault. The Queen of the Night, Monostatos and the ladies lurk beneath the temple, plotting Sarastro's overthrow. At a mighty crash of thunder they vanish into the earth, and the scene is transformed as if into the sun itself. Tamino and Pamina are transfigured in priestly robes. Sarastro stands exalted, and all celebrate the victory of light over darkness.

Erster Aufzug   Act one

ERSTER AUFTRITT

SCENE 1

Felsige Gegend, hie und da mit Bäumen uberwachsen. Auf beiden Seiten Berge nebst einem Tempel.
Tamino kommt in einem prächtigen japanischen Jagdkleide von einem Felsen herunter, mit einem Bogen, aber ohne Pfeil. Eine Schlange verfolgt ihn.

A rocky region with trees growing here and there: mountains on either side and a nearby temple.
Tamino in splendid Japanese hunting costume comes down from a rock, carrying a bow but no arrows: he is pursued by a serpent.

1. INTRODUKTION

1. INTRODUCTION

TAMINO
Zu Hilfe! Zu Hilfe! Sonst bin ich verloren,
Der listigen Schlange zum Opfer erkoren!
Barmherzige Götter! Schon nahet sie sich!
Ach, rettet mich! Ach, schützet mich!

TAMINO
Help! , Help, or I am lost, marked
down as this slippery serpent's prey!
Merciful gods! It is gaining on me!
Ah, save me! Protect me!

(Er fällt in Ohnmacht; sogleich öffnet sich die Pforte des Tempels, drei verschleierte Damen kommen herein, jede mit einem silbernen Wurfspiess.)

(He falls in a swoon. The door of the temple immediately opens, and three veiled ladies enter, each with a silver spear.)

DIE DREI DAMEN
Stirb, Ungeheuer, durch unsre Macht!
(Sie durchbohren die Schlange)
Triumph! Triumph! Sie ist vollbracht,
Die Heldentat! Er ist befreit
Durch unsres Armes Tapferkeit!

THE THREE LADIES
Die, monster, by our might!
(They transfix the serpent with their spears)
Victory! Triumph! The doughty deed is done! He is freed by the valour of our arm!

ERSTE DAME
(Tamino betrachtend)
Ein holder Jüngling, sanft und schön!

1st LADY
(gazing at Tamino)
A handsome youth, gentle and fair!

ZWEITE DAME
So schön, als ich noch nie gesehn!

2nd LADY
Fairer than I have ever seen!

DRITTE DAME
Ja, ja! Gewiss, zum Malen schön!

3rd LADY
Yes indeed! Handsome as a picture!

DIE DREI DAMEN
Würd' ich mein Herz der Liebe weihn,
So müsst' es dieser Jügling sein.
Lasst uns zu unsrer Fürstin eilen,
Ihr diese Nachricht zu erteilen:
Vielleicht, dass dieser schöne Mann
Die vor'ge Ruh ihr geben kann.

THE THREE LADIES
If my heart were given over to love
it would certainly be to this youth.
Let us hasten to our Queen
to acquaint her with this news:
perhaps this handsome young man
can restore her lost peace.

ERSTE DAME
So geht und sagt es ihr,
Ich bleib indessen hier.

1st LADY
Then go and tell her,
While I wait here.

ZWEITE DAME
Nein, nein! Geht ihr nur hin,
Ich wache hier für ihn!

2nd LADY
No, no! You go,
While I watch over him.

DRITTE DAME
Nein, nein! Das kann nicht sein,
Ich schütze ihn allein.

3rd LADY
No, no! That shall not be:
I alone will guard him.

ERSTE DAME
Ich bleib indessen hier!

1st LADY
I'll wait here!

ZWEITE DAME
Ich wache hier für ihn!

2nd LADY
I'll watch over him!

DRITTE DAME
Ich schütze ihn allein!

3rd LADY
I alone will guard him!

ERSTE DAME
Ich bleibe!

1st LADY
I'll wait!

ZWEITE DAME
Ich wache!

2nd LADY
I'll watch!

DRITTE DAME
Ich schütze!

3rd LADY
I'll guard!

DIE DREI DAMEN
Ich, ich, ich!
(jede für sich)
Ich sollte fort? Ei, ei! Wie fein!
Sie wären gern bei ihm allein.
Nein, nein, das kann nicht sein!

THE THREE LADIES
I, I, I!
(each to herself)
I should go? Indeed! The very idea!
They'd like to be alone with him.
No, no, that cannot be!

Was wollte ich darum nicht geben,
Könnt ich mit diesem Jüngling leben,
Hätt ich ihn doch so ganz allein!
Doch keine geht, es kann nicht sein!
Am besten ist es nun, ich geh.
(zusammen)
Du Jüngling, schön und liebevoll,
Du trauter Jüngling, lebe wohl,
Bis ich dich wieder seh!

*(Sie gehen alle drei zur Pforte des
Tempels ab, die sich selbst öffnet
und schliesst.)*

TAMINO
(erwacht)
Wo bin ich? Ist's Phantasie, dass ich
noch lebe? Oder hat eine höhere Macht
mich gerettet? – Die Schlange tot zu
meinen Füssen? – Was hör'ich? Eine
seltsame Gestalt naht sich dem Tal.

(versteckt sich hinter einem Baum)

ZWEITER AUFTRITT

*Papageno kommt während des Vorspiels
einen Fuss-Steig herunter, hat auf dem
Rücken eine grosse Vogelsteige, worin
verschiedene Vögel sind. Mit beiden
Händen hält er ein Faunen-Flötchen.*

2. ARIE

PAPAGENO
Der Vogelfänger bin ich ja,
Stets lustig, heissa, hopsassa!
Ich Vogelfänger bin bekannt
Bei alt und jung im ganzen Land.
Weiss mit dem Locken unzugehn
Und mich aufs Pfeifen zu verstehn.
Drum kann ich froh und lustig sein,
Denn alle Vögel sind ja mein.

Der Vogelfänger bin ich ja,
Stets lustig, heissa, hopsassa!
Ich Vogelfänger bin bekannt
Bei alt und jung im ganzen Land.
Ein Netz für Mädchen möchte ich,
Ich fing sie dutzendweis für mich!

What would I not give
to be able to live with this youth
and have him entirely to myself!
But no one will go: this is not
possible! It is best that I should go.
(together)
O fair and lovely youth,
dear youth, farewell
until we meet again!

*(exeunt all three by the door
of the Temple, which opens and
shuts by itself.)*

TAMINO
(recovering consciousness)
Where am I? Am I dreaming that I'm
alive? Or has a higher power rescued
me? – The serpent dead at my feet?
– What do I hear? A strange figure
is approaching the valley

(He hides behind a tree)

SCENE 2

*During the introduction Pagageno
enters down a footpath: he carries
on his back a large birdcage with
several birds in it. He holds a set of
panpipes in his hands.*

2. ARIA

PAPAGENO
The birdcatcher am I,
always merry and bright, tra la!
As a birdcatcher I'm known
to young and old throughout the
land. I know how to set traps,
and make myself understood on my
pipes. So I can be happy and free,
for all these birds belong to me.

The birdcatcher am I,
always merry and bright, tra la!
As a birdcatcher I'm known
to young and old throughout the
land. If I could spread a net for girls
I'd catch dozens for myself!

Dann sperrte ich sie bei mir ein,
Und alle Mädchen wären mein.

Wenn alle Mädchen wären mein,
So tauschte ich brav Zucker ein:
Die, welche mir am liebsten wär,
Der gäb ich gleich den Zucker her.
Und küsste sie mich zärtlich dann,
Wär sie mein Weib und ich ihr Mann.
Sie schlief an meiner Scitc ein,
Ich wiegte wie ein Kind sie ein.

*(Pfeift, will nacht der Arie nach der
Pforte gehen.)*

TAMINO
He da!

PAPAGENO
Was da!

TAMINO
Sag mir, du lustiger Freund, wer du
bist?

PAPAGENO
Wer ich bin? (Dumme Frage!) Ein Mensch,
wie du. Wenn ich dich nun fragte, wer du
bist?

TAMINO
So würde ich dir antworten: Mein Vater
ist ein Fürst, der über viele Länder und
Menschen herrscht; darum nennt man mich
mich Prinz.

PAPAGENO
Länder? Menschen? Prinz? — Sag du mir
zuvor: gibt's ausser diesen Bergen auch
noch Länder und Menschen?

TAMINO
Viele Tausende!

PAPAGENO
Da liess sich eine Spekulation mit meinen
Vögeln machen.

TAMINO
Nun sag du mir, wie nennt man
eigentlich diese Gegend? Wer beherrscht
sie?

I'd cage them up along with me
and all the girls would belong to me.

If all the girls belonged to me
I'd barter them for sugar,
and give that sugar straight away
to her that pleased me most.
And then she'd kiss me tenderly
and be my wife; I'd be her man;
she'd sleep at my side
and I'd cradle her like a child.

*(He pipes, and after the aria is about
to go towards the temple door.)*

TAMINO
Hey there!

PAPAGENO
Who's that?

TAMINO
Tell me, my merry friend, who are
you?

PAPAGENO
Who am I? (Silly question!) A man,
like yourself. Suppose I asked who
you were?

TAMINO
I'd answer: My father is a king who
rules over many lands and peoples,
so I am called a
prince.

PAPAGENO
Lands? Peoples? Prince? — Tell me
then, are there other lands and
peoples beyond these mountains?

TAMINO
Thousands and thousands!

PAPAGENO
I could do business there with my
birds.

TAMINO
Now tell me, what is this place
called? Who is its
ruler?

36

PAPAGENO

Das kann ich dir ebensowenig
beantworten, als ich weiss, wie ich auf die
Welt gekommen bin. Ich weiss nur so viel,
dass nicht weit von hier meine
Strohhütte steht, die mich vor Regen und
Kälte schützt.

TAMINO

Aber wie lebst du?

PAPAGENO

Von Essen und Trinken, wie alle
Menschen.

TAMINO

Wodurch erhältst du das?

PAPAGENO

Durch Tausch. Ich fange für die
sternflammende Königin und ihre Damen
verschiedene Vögel; dafür erhalt ich
täglich Speis und Trank von ihr.

TAMINO

Sternflammende Königin!
(für sich)
Wenn es gar die Königin der Nacht wäre!
(laut)
Sag,mir, guter Freund, warst du schon so
glücklich, sie zu sehen?

PAPAGENO

Sehen? Die sternflammende Königin
sehen? Wenn du noch einmal mit einer
solchen albernen Frage an mich kommst,
so sperr ich dich, so wahr ich Papageno
heisse, wie einen Gimpel in mein
Vogelhaus, verhandle dich dann mit
meinen übrigen Vögeln an die nächtliche
Königin und ihre Damen, dann mögen sie
dich meinetwegen seiden oder braten.
Welcher Sterbliche kann sich rühmen, sie
je gesehen zu haben?
(für sich)
Wie er mich so starr anblickt!
(laut)
Warum siehst du so verdächtig nach
mir?

PAPAGENO

I can answer that about as well as I
can say how I came into the world.
All I know is that my straw hut,
that shelters me from rain and cold,
isn't far from
here.

TAMINO

But how do you live?

PAPAGENO

By eating and drinking, like all
men.

TAMINO

How do you come by that?

PAPAGENO

By trading. I catch various birds for
the star-blazing Queen and her
ladies, and in return I get food and
drink every day.

TAMINO

Star-blazing Queen!
(aside)
Could that be the Queen of Night?
(aloud)
Tell me, my friend, have you ever
been so fortunate as to see her?

PAPAGENO

See her? See the star-blazing Queen?
If you put such an idiotic question
to me again, as sure as my name's
Papageno I'll shut you in my birdcage like a bullfinch and trade you
with my other birds to the Queen
of Night and her ladies, and they
can boil or roast you, for all I
care. What mortal man can claim
ever to have seen
her?
(aside)
How he stares at me!
(aloud)
Why do you look at me so
suspiciously?

37

TAMINO
Weil ich zweifle, ob du ein Mensch bist.
Nach deinen Federn, die dich bedecken,
halt ich dich . . .

(geht auf ihn zu)

PAPAGENO
Doch für einem Vogel? – Bleib zurück,
sag ich, denn ich habe Riesenkraft!

TAMINO
Riesenkraft?
(Er sieht auf die Schlange)
Dann warst du wohl gar mein Erretter,
der diese böse Schlange getötet hat?

PAPAGENO
Schlange?
*(sieht sich um, weicht zitternd einige
Schritte zurück)*

TAMINO
Aber wie hast du dieses Ungeheuer
bekämpft? Du bist ohne Waffen!

PAPAGENO
Brauch' keine! Bei mir ist ein starker
Druck mit der Hand mehr als Waffen.

TAMINO
Du hast sie also erdrosselt?

PAPAGENO
Erdrosselt!

DRITTER AUFTRITT

Die drei Damen: die Vorigen

DIE DREI DAMEN
Papageno! Papageno! Papageno!

PAPAGENO
Aha, das geht mich an!

TAMINO
Wer sind diese Damen?

TAMINO
Because I'm not sure if you are a
man. From your feathers I'd take
you for . . .

(goes towards him)

PAPAGENO
Not for a bird? Stand back, I say,
for I have a giant's strength!

TAMINO
A giant's strength?
(He looks at the serpent)
Then perhaps it was you who saved
me and killed the terrible serpent?

PAPAGENO
Serpent?
*(He looks around and retreats a few
steps, trembling)*

TAMINO
But how did you overcome this
monster? You have no weapons!

PAPAGENO
I don't need any! The strength of
my grip is better than a weapon.

TAMINO
So you strangled it?

PAPAGENO
Strangled it!

SCENE 3

Enter the three ladies

THE THREE LADIES
Papageno! Papageno! Papageno!

PAPAGENO
Ah! I'm done for!

TAMINO
Who are these ladies?

PAPAGENO
Wer sie eigentlich sind, weiss ich selbst
nicht. Ich weiss nur so viel, dass sie mir
täglich meine Vögel abnehmen und mir
dafür Wein, Zuckerbrot und süsse Feigen
bringen.

TAMINO
Sie sind vermutlich sehr schön?

PAPAGENO
Ich denke nicht! Denn wenn sie schön
wären, würden sie ihre Gesichter nicht
bedecken.

DIE DREI DAMEN
(drohend)
Papageno!

PAPAGENO
Sei still! Sie drohen mir schon.
Du fragst, ob sie schön sind, und ich kann
dir darauf nichts antworten, als dass ich
in meinem Leben nichts Reizenderes sah.
Jetzt werden sie bald wieder gut werden.

DIE DREI DAMEN
(drohend)
Papageno!

PAPAGENO
Was muss ich denn heute verbrochen haben,
das sie so aufgebracht wider mich sind?
Hier, meine Schönen, übergeb ich meine
Vögel.

ERSTE DAME
*(reicht ihm eine schöne Bouteille
Wasser)*
Dafür schickt dir unsere Fürstin heute statt
Wein reines, helles Wasser.

ZWEITE DAME
Und statt Zuckerbrot, diesen Stein. Ich
wünsche, dass er dir wohl bekommen möge.

PAPAGENO
Was? Steine soll ich fressen?

PAPAGENO
I don't know exactly who they are.
I only know that each day they take
away my birds and bring me wine,
sweetmeats and sweet figs in
exchange.

TAMINO
I presume they're very beautiful?

PAPAGENO
I doubt it — for if they were
beautiful they wouldn't veil
their faces.

THE THREE LADIES
(threateningly)
Papageno!

PAPAGENO
Hush! They're threatening me.
You asked if they were beautiful:
I can only answer that in all my life
I've seen nothing more lovely. Now
they'll be all right again.

THE THREE LADIES
(threateningly)
Papageno!

PAPAGENO
What can I have done wrong today
to make them so angry with me?
Here, fair ladies, let me give you my
birds.

1st LADY
*(handing him a beautiful flask
filled with water)*
For that, our Queen sends you today, instead of wine, pure cold water.

2nd LADY
And instead of sweetmeats this
stone. I hope you enjoy it.

PAPAGENO
What? Am I to eat stones?

DRITTE DAME
Und statt der süssen Feigen schlage ich dir dies goldene Schloss vor den Mund.

(Sie schlägt ihm ein Schloss vor.)

PAPAGENO
Hm!

ERSTE DAME
Du willst vermutlich wissen, warum die Fürstin dich heute so wunderbar bestraft?

PAPAGENO
Hm!

ZWEITE DAME
Damit du künftig nie mehr Fremde belügst!

DRITTE DAME
Und dich nie mehr der Heldentaten rühmest, die anderen vollzogen haben.

ERSTE DAME
Sag! Hast du diese Schlange bekämpft?

PAPAGENO
Hm!

ZWEITE DAME
Wer denn also?

DRITTE DAME
Wir waren's, Jüngling, die dich befreiten.

ZWEITE DAME
Zittre nicht; dich erwartet Freude und Entzücken.

ERSTE DAME
Hier, dies schickt dir die grosse Fürstin; es ist das Bildnis ihrer Tochter. Findest du, dass diese Züge dir nicht gleichgültig sind . . .

3rd LADY
And instead of sweet figs I'm to close your lips with this golden padlock.

(She claps a padlock on him.)

PAPAGENO
Hm!

1st LADY
You'd probably like to know why the Queen punishes you so strangely today?

PAPAGENO
Hm!

2nd LADY
So that you won't tell any more lies to strangers!

3rd LADY
And so you won't boast of heroic deeds which others performed.

1st LADY
Tell us, did you fight this serpent?

PAPAGENO
Hm!

2nd LADY
Then who did?

3rd LADY
It was we, noble youth, who saved you.

2nd LADY
Do not be afraid: joy and rapture await you.

1st LADY
The great Queen sends you this: it is a portrait of her daughter. If you find that her features do not leave you indifferent . . . .

DRITTE DAME	3rd LADY
. . . dann ist Glück, Ehr' und Ruhm dein Los.	. . . then fortune, honour and fame are your lot.
DIE DREI DAMEN	THE THREE LADIES
Auf wiedersehen.	Farewell.
ZWEITE DAME	2nd LADY
Adieu, Monsieur Papageno!	Goodbye, Papageno!
ERSTE DAME	1st LADY
Nicht zu hastig getrunken!	Don't drink too fast!
(Sie gehen alle drei ab)	*(Exeunt all three)*

VIERTER AUFTRITT / SCENE 4

Tamino, Papageno

3. ARIE / 3. ARIA

TAMINO	TAMINO
Dies Bildnis ist bezaubernd schön,	This portrait is more enchanting,
Wie noch kein Auge je gesehn!	more lovely, than ever eye beheld!
Ich fühl es, wie dies Götterbild	I feel this divine image
Mein Herz mit neuer Regung füllt.	filling my heart with a new emotion,
Dies Etwas kann ich zwar nicht nennen,	something I can scarcely name
Doch fühl ich's hier wie Feuer brennen.	but can feel burning here like fire.
Soll die Empfindung Liebe sein?	Can this sensation be love?
Ja, ja! Die Liebe ist's allein!	Yes, yes! It can only be love!
O wenn ich sie nur finden könnte!	O if I could only find her!
O wenn sie doch schon vor mir stände!	O if she only stood before me!
Ich würde – würde – warm und rein –	I'd – I'd – warm and pure –
Was würde ich?	What would I do?
Ich würde sie voll Entzücken	I'd clasp her in all tenderness
An diesen heissen Busen drücken,	close to my burning heart
Und ewig wäre sie dann mein.	and she'd be mine for ever.

FÜNFTER AUFTRITT / SCENE 5

Die drei Damen, die Vorigen / *Enter the three ladies*

ERSTE DAME	1st LADY
Rüste dich mit Mut und Standhaftigkeit, schöner Jüngling!	Arm yourself with courage and steadfastness, fair youth!
Die Fürstin . . .	The Queen . . .
ZWEITE DAME	2nd LADY
. . . hat mir aufgetragen, dir zu sagen . . .	. . . has commanded me to say . . .

41

DRITTE DAME . . . dass der Weg zu deinem künftigen Glück nunmehr gebahnt sei.	**3rd LADY** . . . that the way to your future lies open before you.
ERSTE DAME Sie hat jedes deiner Worte gehört. Sie hat . . hat . . .	**1st LADY** She has heard your every word. She has . . .
ZWEITE DAME . . . Jeden Zug in deinem Gesicht gelesen. Ja noch mehr, ihr mütterliches Herz . . .	**2nd LADY** . . . read your feelings in your face. And her loving maternal heart . . .
DRITTE DAME . . . Hat beschlossen; dich ganz glücklich zu machen. Hat dieser Jüngling, sprach sie, auch so viel Mut und Tapferkeit, als er zärtlich ist, so ist meine Tochter Pamina gerettet.	**3rd LADY** . . . has resolved to make you supremely happy. If this youth, she said, has as much courage and valour as he has tenderness, then my Pamina is saved.
TAMINO Gerettet? Pamina?	**TAMINO** Saved? Pamina?
ZWEITE DAME Der Name der Tochter der Königin der Nacht.	**2nd LADY** That is the name of the Queen of Night's daughter.
ERSTE DAME Ein mächtiger, böser Dämon hat sie ihr entrissen.	**1st LADY** A powerful, evil demon has carried her away.
TAMINO Entrissen? Wie ist sein Name?	**TAMINO** Carried her away? What is his name?
DIE DREI DAMEN Sarastro!	**THE THREE LADIES** Sarastro!
TAMINO Wo ist sein Aufenthalt?	**TAMINO** Where does he dwell?
ZWEITE DAME Sehr nahe an unseren Bergen lebt er. Seine Burg ist prachtvoll und sorgsam bewacht.	**2nd LADY** He lives very near our mountains. His castle is magnificent and closely guarded.
TAMINO Kommt, Mädchen, führt mich! Pamina sei gerettet! — Ihr Götter, was ist das?	**TAMINO** Come, ladies, lead me there! Pamina shall be saved! — Ye gods, what is that?
(Donner)	*(Thunder)*

42

DIE DREI DAMEN	THE THREE LADIES
Die Königin! Sie kommt!	The Queen! She is coming!

VERWANDLUNG / **TRANSFORMATION**

Die Berge teilen sich auseinander / *The mountains open*

SECHSTER AUFTRITT / SCENE 6

Die Königin sitzt auf einem Thron, welcher mit transparenten Sternen geziert ist. Vorige

The Queen of Night siting on a throne decorated with transparent stars, the afore-mentioned

4. REZITATIV UND ARIE / 4. RECITATIVE AND ARIA

KÖNIGIN DER NACHT / QUEEN OF NIGHT

O zitt're nicht, mein lieber Sohn!	Have no fear, my dear boy!
Du bist ja schuldlos, weise, fromm.	For you are innocent, wise, gentle.
Ein Jüngling, so wie du, vermag am besten,	A youth like you may best console
Dies tief gebeugte Mutterherz zu trösten.	a sorely afflicted mothers's heart.
Zum Leiden bin ich auserkoren,	To sorrow I am doomed,
Denn meine Tochter fehlet mir;	for I have lost my daughter;
Durch sie ging all mein Glück verloren:	all my joy has gone with her:
Ein Bösewicht entfloh mit ihr.	a villain carried her away.
Noch seh ich ihr Zittern,	I still can see her trembling
Mit bangem Erschüttern,	in fearful terror,
Ihr ängstliches Beben,	her anguished fright,
Ihr schüchternes Streben.	her timid struggles.
Ich musste sie mir rauben sehen:	I had to watch her being taken:
"Ach helft." war alles, was sie sprach;	"O help!" was all she said;
Allein, vergebens war ihr Flehen,	in vain was all her pleading,
Denn meine Hilfe war zu schwach.	for my help was too weak.
Du wirst sie zu befreien gehen,	You shall go to free her,
Du wirst der Tochter Retter sein.	you shall be my daughter's rescuer;
Und werd ich dich als Sieger sehen,	and when I see you here victorious
So sei sie dann auf ewig dein.	she shall be yours for ever.

(Mit den drei Damen ab) / *(She and the three ladies disappear)*

VERWANDLUNG / **TRANSFORMATION**

Die Berge schliessen sich wieder / *The mountains close again*

SIEBENTER AUFTRITT / SCENE 7

Tamino, Papageno / *Tamino, Papageno*

TAMINO
Ist es denn Wirklichkeit, was ich sah?

(Papageno tritt vor ihn hin)

5. QUINTETT

PAPAGENO
(deuct traurig auf das Schloss am Munde)
Hm, hm, hm, hm!

TAMINO
Der Arme kann von Strafe sagen,
Denn seine Sprache ist dahin.

PAPAGENO
Hm, hm, hm, hm!

TAMINO
Ich kann nichts tun, als dich beklagen,
Weil ich zu schwach zu helfen bin.

PAPAGENO
Hm, hm, hm, hm!

ACHTER AUFTRITT

Die drei Damen, die Vorigen

ERSTE DAME
(zu Papageno)
Die Königin begnadigt dich,
Erlässt die Strafe dir durch mich.

(Sie nimmt ihm das Schloss vom Munde)

PAPAGENO
Nun plaudert Papageno wieder.

ZWEITE DAME
Ja, plaud're! Lüge nur nicht wieder!

PAPAGENO
Ich lüge nimmermehr. Nein! Nein!

DIE DREI DAMEN
Dies Schloss soll deine Warnung sein!

TAMINO
Was what I saw really true?

(Papageno approaches him)

5. QUINTET

PAPAGENO
(sadly pointing to the padlock on his lips)
Hm, hm, hm, hm!

TAMINO
Poor wretch, his plight is audible,
for his tongue is locked up.

PAPAGENO
Hm, hm, hm, hm!

TAMINO
I can do nothing but pity you,
for I have no means of helping.

PAPAGENO
Hm, hm, hm, hm!

SCENE 8

Enter the three ladies

1st LADY
(to Papageno)
The Queen has forgiven you,
and through me remits your sentence.

(She removes the padlock from his lips)

PAPAGENO
Now Papageno can chatter again.

2nd LADY
Chatter, yes, but no more lies!

PAPAGENO
I'll never lie again. No, no!

THE THREE LADIES
This padlock shall serve as warning!

PAPAGENO
Dies Schloss soll meine Warnung sein!

ALLE
Bekämen doch die Lügner alle
Ein solches Schloss vor ihren Mund,
Statt Hass, Verleumdung, schwarzer Galle,
Bestünde Lieb' und Bruderbund.

ERSTE DAME
(Gibt Tamino eine goldne Flöte)
O Prinz, nimm dies Geschenk von mir!
Dies sendet unsre Fürstin dir.
Die Zauberflöte wird dich schützen,
Im grössten Unglück unterstützen.

DIE DREI DAMEN
Hiermit kannst du allmächtig handeln,
Der Menschen Leidenschaft verwandeln:
Der Traurige wird freudig sein,
Den Hagestolz nimmt Liebe ein.

ALLE
Oh, so eine Flöte ist mehr als Gold und
Kronen wert,
Denn durch sie wird Menschenglück
und Zufriedenheit vermehrt.

PAPAGENO
Nun, ihr schönen Frauenzimmer,
Darf ich — so empfehl ich mich.

DIE DREI DAMEN
Dich empfehlen kannst du immer,
Doch bestimmt die Fürstin dich,
Mit dem Prinzen ohn' Verweilen
Nach Sarastros Burg zu eilen.

PAPAGENO
Nein, dafür bedank ich mich!
Von euch selbsten hörte ich,
Dass er wie ein Tigertier.
Sicher liess ohn' alle Gnaden
Mich Sarastro rupfen, braten,
Setze mich den Hunden für.

DIE DREI DAMEN
Dich schützt der Prinz, trau ihm allein!
Dafür sollst du sein Diener
sein.

PAPAGENO
This padlock shall serve as warning!

ALL
If all liars thus received
padlocks for their lips,
instead of hate, slander and bile,
love and brotherhood would prevail.

1st LADY
(giving Tamino a golden flute)
O prince, take this gift from me:
it is sent you by our Queen.
The magic flute will protect you
and sustain you in direst straits.

THE THREE LADIES
With this you have limitless power
to transform men's passions:
the sad will become joyful,
the misogynist will turn to love.

ALL
Yes, such a flute is worth more than
gold and crowns, for by it mankind's
happiness and content are
increased.

PAPAGENO
Now, lovely ladies, with your
permission I'll take my leave.

THE THREE LADIES
You may take your leave indeed,
but our Queen commands you
unhesitatingly to hasten with the
prince to Sarastro's castle.

PAPAGENO
No, thanks all the same!
I've heard from your own lips
that he's like a wild tiger.
Sarastro would certainly without
mercy pluck and roast me
or set his dogs on me.

THE THREE LADIES
The prince will protect you; just
trust him! In return you shall serve
him.

45

PAPAGENO
(für sich)
Das doch der Prinz beim Teufel wäre!
Mein Leben ist mir lieb;
Am Ende schleicht, bei meiner Ehre,
Er von mir wie ein Dieb.

PAPAGENO
(aside)
Devil take the prince!
My life is dear to me;
at the end, I'll warrant,
he'll give me the slip like a thief.

ERSTE DAME
(gibt Papageno ein Kästchen mit ein Glockenspiel)
Hier nimm dies Kleinod, es ist dein.

1st LADY
(giving Papageno a box with a chime of bells)
Take this box here: it is yours.

PAPAGENO
Werd ich sie auch wohl spielen können?

PAPAGENO
Can I play them too?

DIE DREI DAMEN
O ganz gewiss! Ja, ja, gewiss!

THE THREE LADIES
O yes, indeed! Yes indeed!

ALLE
Silberglöckchen, Zauberflöten
Sind zu eurem Schutz vonnöten.
Lebet wohl, wir wollen gehn,
Lebet wohl, auf wiedersehn!

ALL
Silver bells and magic flute
will assure your safety.
Farewell; we must go;
farewell till we meet again!

TAMINO
Doch, schöne Damen, saget an:

TAMINO
But, fair ladies, tell us . . .

PAPAGENO
Wie man die Burg wohl finden kann?

PAPAGENO
. . . how shall we find the castle?

TAMINO, PAPAGENO
Wie man die Burg wohl finden kann?

TAMINO, PAPAGENO
How shall we find the castle?

DIE DREI DAMEN
Drei Knaben, jung, schön, hold und weise,
Umschweben euch auf eurer Reise;
Sie werden eure Führer sein,
Folgt ihrem Rate ganz allein.

THE THREE LADIES
Three boys, young, fair, gentle and
wise, will attend you on your
journey; they will be your guides:
follow their counsel only.

TAMINO, PAPAGENO
Drei Knaben, jung, schön, hold und weise,
Umschweben uns auf unsrer Reise.

TAMINO, PAPAGENO
Three boys, young, fair, gentle and
wise, will attend us on our journey.

ALLE
So lebet wohl! Wir wollen gehn,
Lebt wohl, lebt wohl! Auf wiedersehn!

ALL
Farewell, for we must go;
farewell till we meet again.

VERWANDLUNG

TRANSFORMATION

Prächtiges Zimmer in Sarastros Palast

A magnificent room in Sarastro's palace

46

NEUNTER AUFTRITT	SCENE 9

Monostatos. Pamina, die von Sklaven her-eingeführt wird

Monostatos. Pamina, brought in by slaves

6. TERZETT

6. TRIO

MONOSTATOS
Du feines Täubchen, nur herein!

MONOSTATOS
Come in, my pretty dove!

PAMINA
O welche Marter! Welche Pein!

PAMINA
O what torment! What anguish!

MONOSTATOS
Verloren ist dein Leben!

MONOSTATOS
Your life is doomed!

PAMINA
Der Tod macht mich nicht beben,
Nur meine Mutter dauert mich;
Sie stirbt vor Gram ganz sicherlich.

PAMINA
Death does not make me flinch;
I grieve only for my mother;
she will surely die of sorrow.

MONOSTATOS
He, Sklaven! Legt ihr Fesseln an!
(Sie legen ihr Fesseln an)
Mein Hass soll dich verderben.

MONOSTATOS
Ho, slaves! Put her in chains!
(They fetter her)
My hatred shall destroy you.

PAMINA
O lass mich lieber sterben,
Weil nichts, Barbar, dich rühren kann!
(Sie sinkt ohnmächtig auf ein Sofa)

PAMINA
O rather let me die, barbarian,
since nothing can soften your heart.
(She falls in a swoon on to a sofa)

MONOSTATOS
Nun fort! Lasst mich bei ihr
allein.
(Die Sklaven gehen ab)

MONOSTATOS
Now away! Leave me alone with
her.
(Exeunt slaves)

ZEHNTER AUFTRITT	SCENE 10

Papageno, die Vorigen

Papageno, the afore-mentioned

PAPAGENO
(von aussen am Fenster, ohne gleich gesehen zu werden)
Wo bin ich wohl? Wo mag ich sein?
Aha, da find ich Leute!
Gewagt, ich geh hinein.
(Geht hinein)
Schön Mädchen, jung und fein,
Viel weisser noch als Kreide!

PAPAGENO
(outside, at the window, without himself being seen)
Where am I then? Where can I be?
Ah, there's somebody!
I'll risk it and go in.
(goes in)
Fair maiden, young and tender,
far whiter than the snow . . .

MONOSTATOS, PAPAGENO
(erschrecken einer über den andern)
Hu! Das ist der Teufel sicherlich!
Hab Mitleid! Verschone mich!
Hu! Hu! Hu!

(Laufen beide ab)

ELFTER AUFTRITT

Papageno, Pamina

PAMINA
(spricht wie im Traum)
Mutter! Mutter! Mutter!
(Sie erholt sich, sieht sich um)
Wie? Noch schlagt dieses Herz? Noch nicht vernichtet? Zu neuen Qualen erwacht! O das ist hart — mir bitterer als der Tod.

PAPAGENO
Bin ich nicht ein Narr, dass ich mich schrecken liess? Es gibt ja schwarze Vögel in der Welt, warum denn nicht auch schwarze Menschen? — Ah, sieh! Hier ist ja Pamina! Du Tochter der nächtlichen Königin . . .

PAMINA
Wer bist du?

PAPAGENO
Ein Abgesandter der sternflammenden Königin.

PAMINA
(freudig)
Meiner Mutter? Oh! Dein Name?

PAPAGENO
Papageno.

PAMINA
Papageno? Papageno? Ich erinnere mich, den Namen oft gehort zu haben, dich selbst aber sah ich nie!

PAPAGENO
Ich dich auch nicht!

MONOSTATOS, PAPAGENO
(terrified at the sight of each other)
Ooh! That is the devil, for sure!
Have mercy! Spare me!
Ooh! Ooh! Ooh!

(Both run away)

SCENE 11

Papageno, Pamina

PAMINA
(as if in a dream)
Oh mother, mother!
(recovering herself and looking about her)
What, is my heart still beating? I'm not dead? Oh, to awake to fresh torments is hard indeed — more bitter to me than death.

PAPAGENO
Aren't I a fool to be so frightened? There are black birds in the world, so why not black men? — Ah now, that must be Pamina! Daughter of the Queen of Night . . .

PAMINA
Who are you?

PAPAGENO
I'm sent by the star-blazing Queen.

PAMINA
(Joyfully)
My mother? What's your name?

PAPAGENO
Papageno.

PAMINA
Papageno? Papageno? Yes, I remember often hearing your name, but I've never seen you before!

PAPAGENO
Nor I you!

48

PAMINA
Du kennst also meine gute, zärtliche Mutter?

PAPAGENO
Wenn du die Tochter der nächtlichen Königin bist — ja!

PAMINA
Oh, ich bin es.

PAPAGENO
Das will ich gleich erkennen.
(Er sieht das Porträt an, welches der Prinz zuvor empfangen und Papageno nun an einem Bande am Halse trägt)
Die Augen schwarz — richtig schwarz: die Lippen rot — richtig rot: blonde Haare — blonde Haare. Alles trifft ein, bis auf Händ' und Füsse. Nach dem Gemälde zu schliessen solltest du weder Hände noch Füsse haben, denn hier sind keine angezeigt.

PAMINA
Erlaube mir — Ja, ich bin's. Wie kam es in deine Hände?

PAPAGENO
Ich liefere deiner Mutter schon seit vielen Jahren alle die schönen Vögel in den Palast. — Heute, als ich im Begriff war, meine Vögel abzugeben, sah ich plötzlich einen Menschen vor mir, der sich Prinz nennen lässt. Kurz: Dieser Prinz hat deine Mutter so eingenommen, das sie ihm dein Bildnis schenkte und ihm befahl, dich zu befreien. Sein Entschluss war so schnell, als seine Liebe zu dir.

PAMINA
Er liebt mich? — Ja, aber, warum säumt er so lange?

PAPAGENO
Mich hat der Prinz vorausgeschickt, um dir seine Ankunft anzukündigen.

PAMINA
So you know my dear sweet mother?

PAPAGENO
If you're the daughter of the Queen of Night, yes!

PAMINA
Oh, I am.

PAPAGENO
We'll soon see.
(He looks at the portrait which the prince had received and which Papageno now carries on a ribbon round his neck)
Black eyes — that's right: red lips — yes, they're red: fair hair — yes, fair. It all corresponds, except for the hands and feet. According to the picture you shouldn't have either hands or feet, for none are shown here.

PAMINA
Allow me — yes, that is I. How did this come into your hands?

PAPAGENO
For many years now I've delivered all kinds of beautiful birds to your mother in the palace. — Today, as I was about to hand over my birds, I suddenly saw before me a man who calls himself a prince. To be brief, your mother was so taken with this prince that she gave him your portrait and commanded him to rescue you. He took his decision as quickly as he had fallen in love with you.

PAMINA
He loves me? Then why does he delay so long?

PAPAGENO
The prince sent me on ahead to say that he's coming.

PAMINA
Du hast viel gewagt! Wenn Sarastro dich hier erblicken sollte . . .

PAPAGENO
So wird mir meine Rückreise erspart. Das kann ich mir denken.

PAMINA
Du hast noch kein Weib, das auf dich wartet?

PAPAGENO
Noch nicht einmal ein Mädchen, viel weniger ein Weib! Ich möchte mir oft alle meine Federn ausrupfen, wenn ich bedenke, dass Papageno noch keine Papagena hat!

PAMINA
Geduld, Freund! Der Himmel wird auch für dich sorgen!

7. DUETT

PAMINA

Bei Männern, welche Liebe fühlen,
Fehlt auch ein gutes Herze nicht.

PAPAGENO
Die süssen Triebe mitzufühlen,
Ist dann der Weiber erste Pflicht.

BEIDE
Wir wollen uns der Liebe freun,
Wir leben durch die Lieb' allein.

PAMINA
Die Lieb' versüsset jede Plage,
Ihr opfert jede Kreatur.

PAPAGENO
Sie würzet unsre Lebenstage,
Sie wirkt im Kreise der Natur.

BEIDE
Ihr hoher Zweck zeigt deutlich an,
Nichts Edler sei, als Weib und Mann.
Mann und Weib, und Weib und Mann,
Reichen an die Gotteit an.

PAMINA
You're very daring! If Sarastro were to see you here . . .

PAPAGENO
I'd be spared the return journey, I'm sure.

PAMINA
Haven't you a wife waiting for you?

PAPAGENO
Not even a sweetheart, much less a wife! I could often pluck out all my feathers when I think that Papageno still has no Papagena!

PAMINA
Patience, my friend! Heaven will look after you too!

7. DUET

PAMINA

Men who feel the call of love
are not lacking in a gentle heart.

PAPAGENO
To share those sweet emotions
is women's first duty.

BOTH
We will rejoice in love
and live for love alone.

PAMINA
Love sweetens every sorrow,
and all creatures pay it homage.

PAPAGENO
It adds spice to our days on earth
and affects the whole of Nature.

BOTH
Its supreme goal is clear:
nothing is nobler than a man and wife. Man and wife, wife and man,
attain to divinity.

VERWANDLUNG	TRANSFORMATION

Ein Hain. Im Grunde der Bühne ist ein schöner Tempel, worauf diese Worte stehen: Tempel der Weisheit. Dieser Tempel führt mit Säulen zu zwei anderen Tempeln; rechts auf dem einen steht: Tempel der Vernunft. Links steht: Tempel der Natur.

A grove. At the back of the scene is a fine temple on which are the words 'Temple of Wisdom'. From this a colonnade leads to two other temples: on the right-hand one is inscribed 'Temple of Reason', on the left 'Temple of Nature'.

ZWÖLFTER AUFTRITT

SCENE 12

Drei Knaben führen den Tamino herein, jeder hat einen silbernen Palmzweig in der Hand

Three boys each carrying a silver palm-branch in his hand lead in Tamino

8. FINALE

8. FINALE

DIE DREI KNABEN
Zum Ziele führt dich diese Bahn,
Doch musst du, Jüngling, männlich siegen.
Drum höre unsre Lehre an:
Sei standhaft, duldsam und verschwiegen!

THE THREE BOYS
This path leads you to your goal, o youth, but you must win through by your manhood. So hark to what we say: be constant, patient and silent!

TAMINO
Ihr holden Kleinen, sagt mir an,
Ob ich Pamina retten kann?

TAMINO
Fair boys, tell me whether I can save Pamina?

DIE DREI KNABEN
Dies kund zu tun, steht uns nicht an:
Sei standhaft, duldsam und verschwiegen!
Bedenke dies: kurz, sei ein Mann,
Dann, Jüngling, wirst du männlich siegen.
(gehen ab)

THE THREE BOYS
It is not for us to make this known.
Be constant, patient and silent!
Reflect on this: in brief, be a man,
then, o youth, you will win through by your manhood.
(exeunt)

REZITATIV

RECITATIVE

TAMINO
Die Weisheitslehre dieser Knaben
Sei ewig mir ins Herz gegraben.
Wo bin ich nun? Was wird mit mir?
Ist dies der Sitz der Götter hier?
Es zeigen die Pforten, es zeigen die Säulen,
Das Klugheit und Arbeit und Künste hier weilen;
Wo Tätigkeit thronet und Müssiggang weicht,

TAMINO
May the wise teaching of these boys be engraved for ever on my heart. Where am I now? What will happen to me? Is this the seat of the gods? The gates and pillars show that prudence, work and art dwell here: where activity reigns and idleness shrinks, no vice can easily hold sway. Boldly I will venture

Erhält seine Herrschaft das Laster nicht
leight.
Ich wage mich mutig zur Pforte hinein,
Die Absicht ist edel und Lauter und rein.
Erzitt're, feiger Bösewicht!
Pamina retten ist mir Pflicht.

*(Er geht an die Pforte zur rechten Seite.
Man hört eine Stimme:)*

PREISTER
Zurück!

TAMINO
Zurück? So wag ich hier mein Glück!

*(Er geht zur linken Pforte: eine Stimme
von innen:)*

PRIESTER
Zurück!

TAMINO
Auch hier ruft man: "Zurück"?
(Er geht zur mittleren Pforte)
Da seh' ich noch eine Tür,
Vielleicht find ich den Eingang hier.

(Er klopft, ein alter Priester erscheint)

SPRECHER
Wo willst du, kühner Fremdling, hin?
Was suchst du hier im Heiligtum?

TAMINO
Der Lieb' und Tugend Eigentum.

SPRECHER
Die Worte sind von hohem Sinn!
Allein, wie willst du diese finden?
Dich leitet Lieb' und Tugend nicht,
Weil Tod und Rache dich entzünden.

TAMINO
Nur Rache für den Bösewicht!

SPRECHER
Den wirst du wohl bei uns nicht finden.

inside the gate; my purpose is
noble, clear and pure. Tremble,
cowardly villain!
I have vowed to rescue Pamina.

*(he goes to the gate on the right. A
voice is heard:)*

PRIEST
Stand back!

TAMINO
Stand back? Then I'll try my luck here!

*(He goes to the gate on the left. A
voice from within:)*

PRIEST
Stand back!

TAMINO
Here too they cry "Stand back"?
(He goes to the centre gate)
I see yet another door:
perhaps I'll find an entrance here.

(He knocks: an elderly priest appears)

SPEAKER
What would you here, bold stranger?
What seek you in this sanctuary?

TAMINO
The realm of love and virtue.

SPEAKER
These words reveal a lofty mind!
How will you find them on your
own? Love and virtue will not lead
you while thoughts of death and
vengeance inflame you.

TAMINO
Vengeance only upon a villain!

SPEAKER
You will not find one here.

TAMINO
Sarastro herrscht in diesen Gründen?

SPRECHER
Ja, ja, Sarastro herrschet hier!

TAMINO
Doch in dem Weisheitstempel nicht?

SPRECHER
Er herrscht im Weisheitstempel
hier.

TAMINO
(will gehen)
So ist denn alles Heuchelei!

SPRECHER
Willst du schon wieder gehn?

TAMINO
Ja, ich will gehn, froh und frei,
Nie euren Tempel sehn!

SPRECHER
Erklär dich näher mir,
Dich täuschet ein Betrug.

TAMINO
Sarastro wohnet hier.
Das ist mir schon genug.

SPRECHER
Wenn du dein Leben liebst,
So rede, bleibe da!
Sarastro hassest du?

TAMINO
Ich hass ihn ewig! Ja!

SPRECHER
Nun gib mir deine Gründe an.

TAMINO
Er ist ein Unmensch, ein Tyrann!

SPRECHER
Ist das, was du gesagt, erwiesen?

TAMINO
Does Sarastro rule in this place?

SPEAKER
Yes indeed, Sarastro is ruler here.

TAMINO
Yet not in the Temple of Wisdom?

SPEAKER
He reigns in the Temple of Wisdom
here.

TAMINO
(makes to leave)
Then everything's hypocrisy!

SPEAKER
Will you go back so soon?

TAMINO
Yes, I will go, gladly and freely,
and never see your Temple!

SPEAKER
Explain yourself further;
some deceit has misled you.

TAMINO
Sarastro dwells here;
that is enough for me.

SPEAKER
If you hold your life dear,
speak up and remain here!
Do you hate Sarastro?

TAMINO
I will always hate him, yes!

SPEAKER
Then give me your reasons.

TAMINO
He is a monster, a tyrant!

SPEAKER
Is there proof of what you say?

TAMINO
Durch ein unglücklich Weib bewiesen,
Das Gram und Jammer niederdrückt.

SPRECHER
Ein Weib hat also dich berückt?
Ein Weib tut wenig, plaudert viel.
Du, Jüngling, glaubst dem Zungenspiel?
O, legte doch Sarastro dir
Die Absicht seiner Handlung für!

TAMINO
Die Absicht ist nur allzu klar!
Riss nicht der Räuber ohn' Erbarmen
Pamina aus der Mutter Armen?

SPRECHER
Ja, Jüngling! Was du sagst, ist wahr.

TAMINO
Wo ist sie, die er uns geraubt?
Man opferte vielleicht sie schon?

SPRECHER
Dir dies zu sagen, teurer Sohn,
Ist jetzund mir noch nicht erlaubt.

TAMINO
Erklär dies Rätsel, täusch' mich nicht.

SPRECHER
Die Zunge bindet Eid und pflicht.

TAMINO
Wann also wird das Dunkel schwinden?

SPRECHER
Sobald dich führt der Freundschaft Hand
Ins Heiligtum zum ew'gen Band.

(geht ab)

TAMINO
(allein)
O ew'ge Nacht! Wann wirst du schwinden?
Wann wird das Licht mein Auge finden?

TAMINO
Proof by an unhappy woman
oppressed with grief and woe.

SPEAKER
So a woman has beguiled you?
Women do little but chatter much.
And you, youth, believe their
wagging tongues? O could Sarastro
reveal the purpose of his actions!

TAMINO
His purpose is all too clear!
Did not the robber ruthlessly tear
Pamina from her mother's arms?

SPEAKER
Yes, young man, what you say is true.

TAMINO
Where is she, whom he stole from us?
Has she perhaps already been
sacrificed?

SPEAKER
I am not yet permitted
to tell you this, my dear son.

TAMINO
Explain this riddle; do not mislead me.

SPEAKER
My duty and my vow bind my tongue.

TAMINO
Then when will this darkness be at
an end?

SPEAKER
As soon as friendship's hand leads
you to the sanctuary's eternal bond.

(exit)

TAMINO
(alone)
O endless night, when will you disperse? When shall light touch my eyes?

CHOR *(von innen)* Bald, bald, Jüngling, oder nie!	CHORUS *(within)* Soon, soon, O youth, or never!
TAMINO Bald, sagt ihr, oder nie? Ihr Unsichtbaren, saget mir, Lebt denn Pamina noch?	TAMINO Soon, you say, or never? You invisible ones, tell me, is Pamina then still alive?
CHOR Pamina lebet noch!	CHORUS Pamina still lives!
TAMINO Sie lebt? Ich danke euch dafür. *(Er nimmt seine Flöte heraus)*	TAMINO She lives? I thank you for those words. *(He takes out his flute)*
O, wenn ich doch imstande wäre, Allmächtige, zu eurer Ehre, Mit jedem Tone meinen Dank zu schildern, Wie er hier entsprang! *(aufs Herz deutend) (Er spielt; sogleich kommen Tiere von allen Arten hervor, ihm zuzuhören. Er hört auf, und sie fliehen.)*	O were I only able, almighty gods, in your honour to express in every note my gratitude as it springs from here! *(indicating his heart) (He plays; at once animals of all kinds come out to listen to him. He stops, and they run away.)*
Wie stark ist nicht dein Zauberton, Weil, holde Flöte, durch dein Spielen Selbst wilde Tiere Freude fühlen. Doch nur Pamina bleibt davon. *(Er spielt)* Pamina! Höre, höre mich! Umsonst! Wo? Ach, wo find ich dich?	How strong must be your magic sway, lovely flute, if at your sound even wild beasts feel joy. But only Pamina is far away. *(He plays)* Pamina! Listen! O hear me! In vain! Where, ah where shall I find you?
PAPAGENO *antwortet von innen mit seinem Flötchen*	PAPAGENO *answers from within on his pipes*
TAMINO Ha, das ist Papagenos Ton! *(Er spielt;* PAPAGENO *antwortet)*	TAMINO Ah, that is Papageno's note! *(He plays;* PAPAGENO *answers)*
TAMINO Vielleicht sah er Pamina schon, Vielleicht eilt sie mit ihm zu mir! Vielleicht führt mich der Ton zu ihr.	TAMINO Perhaps he's already seen Pamina, perhaps she's hurrying to me with him, perhaps the sound will guide me to them!
(Er eilt ab)	*(He hurries off)*

DREIZEHNTER AUFTRITT

Pamina, Papageno

PAMINA, PAPAGENO
Schnelle Füsse, rascher Mut
Schützt vor Feindes List und Wut.
Fänden wir Tamino doch,
Sonst erwischen sie uns noch!

PAMINA
Holder Jüngling!

PAPAGENO
Stille, stille, ich kann's besser!

(Er pfeift)

TAMINO
antwortet von innen auf seiner Flöte

PAMINA, PAPAGENO
Welche Freude ist wohl grösser?
Freund Tamino hört uns schon.
Hierher kam der Flötenton.
Welch ein Glück, wenn ich ihn finde!
Nur geschwinde! Nur geschwinde!

(Wollen hineingehen)

VIERZEHNTER AUFTRITT

Monostatos, Sklaven, die Vorigen

MONOSTATOS
(ihrer spottend)
Nur geschwinde! Nur geschwinde!
Ha, hab ich euch noch erwischt?
Nur herbei mit Stahl und Eisen;
Wart, ich will euch Mores weisen.
Den Monostatos berücken!
Nur berbei mit Band und Stricken!
He, ihr Sklaven, kommt herbei!

PAMINA, PAPAGENO
Ach, nun ist's mit uns vorbei!

MONOSTATOS
He, ihr Sklaven, kommt herbei!

56

SCENE 13

Pamina, Papageno

PAMINA, PAPAGENO
Swiftness of foot and boldness of
heart will save us from our
adversary's cunning and rage. But let
us find Tamino or we shall be
recaptured!

PAMINA
Fair Youth!

PAPAGENO
Hush! I can do better!

(He pipes)

TAMINO
answers from within on his flute

PAMINA, PAPAGENO
What joy could be greater?
Our friend Tamino has heard us:
the sound of his flute reached us.
What happiness if I find him!
Quickly! Quickly!

(They are about to go)

SCENE 14

*Monostatos, slaves, the
afore-mentioned*

MONOSTATOS
(mocking them)
Quickly, quickly!
Ah, have I caught you?
Just bring irons and chains:
wait, I'll teach you how to behave.
You would cheat Monostatos?
Just bring bonds and fetters!
Ho, slaves, come forth!

PAMINA, PAPAGENO
Ah, all is lost!

MONOSTATOS
Ho! slaves, come forth!

(Sklaven kommen mit Fesseln)	*(Slaves enter with fetters)*

PAPAGENO
Wer viel wagt, gewinnt oft viel!
Komm, du schönes Glockenspiel,
Lass die Glöckchen klingen,
Dass die Ohren ihnen singen.

*(Er spielt auf seinem Glockenspiel.
Sogleich tanzen und singen Monostatos
und die Sklaven)*

MONOSTATOS, SKLAVEN
Das klinget so herrlich,
Das klinget so schön!
Larala la la larala!
Nie hab ich so etwas gehört und gesehn!
Larala la la larala!

(Sie tanzen ab)

PAMINA, PAPAGENO
Könnte jeder brave Mann
Solche Glöckchen finden,
Seine Feinde würden dann
Ohne Mühe schwinden,
Und er lebte ohne sie
In der besten Harmonie!
Nur der Freundschaft Harmonie
Mildert die Beschwerden;
Ohne diese Sympathie
Ist kein Glück auf Erden!

STIMMEN
(von innen)
Es lebe Sarastro, Sarastro lebe!

PAPAGENO
Was soll das bedeuten? Ich zittre, ich
bebe.

PAMINA
O Freund, nun ist's um uns getan,
Dies kündigt den Sarastro an.

PAPAGENO
O wär ich eine Maus,
Wie wollt ich mich verstecken!
Wär ich so klein wie Schnecken!
So kröch ich in mein Haus.
Mein Kind, was werden wir nun sprechen?

PAPAGENO
Nothing venture, nothing win!
Come, pretty chime of bells,
let your little bells tinkle,
that all ears may ring.

*(He plays on the chime of bells, At
once Monostatos and the slaves
begin to dance and sing)*

MONOSTATOS, SLAVES
That sounds so pretty,
that sounds so lovely!
Larala la la larala!
Never have I seen or heard the like!
Larala la la larala!

(They dance off)

PAMINA, PAPAGENO
If every good man
owned bells like these,
his foes would then
fade away effortlessly,
and he would live without them
in perfect harmony!
Only friendship's harmony
softens hardship;
without this sympathy
there is no happiness on earth!

VOICES
(from within)
Long live Sarastro!

PAPAGENO
What does that mean? I tremble and
quake.

PAMINA
Friend, all is over for us;
this heralds Sarastro's approach.

PAPAGENO
O that I were a mouse —
how I would hide!
If I were only as small as a snail!
I'd crawl into my house.
Child, what can we say now?

57

PAMINA
Die Wahrheit, wär sie auch Verbrechen!

PAMINA
The truth, though it be held a crime!

FÜNFZEHNTER AUFTRITT

*Zug von Gefolge; zuletzt fährt Sarastro
auf einem Triumphwagen heraus, der von
sechs Löwen gezogen wird.
Vorige.*

CHOR
Es lebe Sarastro, Sarastro soll leben!
Er ist es, dem wir uns mit Freuden ergeben!
Stets mög er des Lebens als Weiser sich
freun.
Er ist inser Abgott, dem alle sich weihn.

*(Dieser Chor wird gesungen, bis Sarastro
aus dem Wagen ist)*

PAMINA
(kniet)
Herr, ich bin zwar Verbrecherin,
Ich wollte deiner Macht entfliehn.
Allein die Schuld liegt nicht an mir:
Der böse Mohr verlangte Liebe;
Darum, o Herr, entfloh ich dir

SARASTRO
Steh auf, erheitre dich, o Liebe!
Denn ohne erst in dich zu dringen,
Weiss ich von deinem Herzen mehr:
Du liebst einen andern sehr.
Zur Liebe will ich dich nicht zwingen,
Doch geb ich dir die Freiheit nicht.

PAMINA
Mich rufet ja des Kindes Pflicht,
Denn meine Mutter . . .

SARASTRO
. . . steht in meiner Macht.
Du würdest um dein Glück gebracht,
Wenn ich dich ihren Händen liesse.

PAMINA
Mir klingt der Muttername süsse!
Sie ist es . . .

SCENE 15

*Sarastro is led on in a triumphal
chariot drawn by six lions,
preceded by his attendants. The
afore-mentioned.*

CHOIR
Long live Sarastro, long may he live!
He it is to whom we gladly dedicate
ourselves! Long may he enjoy life in
his wisdom. He is our mentor, to
whom we are devoted!

*(This chorus is sung until Sarastro
alights from the chariot)*

PAMINA
(kneeling)
Lord, I must confess my sin:
I sought to escape from your power.
But the fault is not wholly mine:
the wicked Moor forced his love on
me, and that is why I was fleeing
from here.

SARASTRO
Arise, and take heart, my dear!
For without even probing
I know the secret of your heart:
you deeply love another.
I will not constrain your love,
yet I will not set you free.

PAMINA
Filial duty summons me,
for my mother . . .

SARASTRO
. . . is in my power.
Your happiness would be at an end
if I let you into her hands.

PAMINA
My mother's name sounds sweet to
me! She is . . .

SARASTRO
... und ein stolzes Weib!
Ein Mann muss eure Herzen leiten,
Denn ohne ihn pflegt jedes Weib
Aus ihrem Wirkungskreis zu schreiten.

SECHZEHNTER AUFTRITT

MONOSTATOS
(führt Tamino hinein)
Nun, stolzer Jüngling, nur hierher,
Hier ist Sarastro, unser Herr.

PAMINA
Er ist's!

TAMINO
Sie ist's!

PAMINA
Ich glaub' es kaum!

TAMINO
Es ist kein Traum!

PAMINA
Es schling' mein Arm sich um ihn her!

TAMINO
Es schling' mein Arm sich um sie her!

PAMINA, TAMINO
Und wenn es auch mein Ende wär!

(Sie umarmen sich)

CHOR
Was soll das heissen?

MONOSTATOS
Welch eine Dreistigkeit!
Gleich auseinander! Das geht zu weit!

*(Er trennt sie, kniet dann vor Sarastro
nieder)*
Dein Sklave liegt zu deinen Füssen!
Lass den verwegnen Frevler büssen!
Bedenk, wie frech der Knabe ist!
(Er zeigt auf Papageno)

SARASTRO
... an arrogant woman!
A man must guide your heart,
for without one every woman seeks
to exceed her rightful place.

SCENE 16

MONOSTATOS
(bringing in Tamino)
Now, proud youth, just come this
way: here is Sarastro, our master.

PAMINA
'Tis he!

TAMINO
'Tis she!

PAMINA
I can scarcely believe it!

TAMINO
This is no dream!

PAMINA
My arms seek to embrace him!

TAMINO
My arms seek to embrace her!

PAMINA, TAMINO
Even if this should mean my death!

(They embrace)

CHORUS
What can this mean?

MONOSTATOS
What effrontery!
Stand apart at once! This goes too
far!

*(He parts them, then kneels before
Sarastro)*
Your slave lies at your feet:
make this audacious sinner suffer!
Consider this fellow's impudence!
(indicating Papageno)

Durch diese seltnen Vogels List
Wollt er Paminen dir entführen.
Allein ich wusst ihn auszuspüren!
Du kennst mich! Meine Wachsamkeit . . .

SARASTRO
. . . verdient, dass man ihr Lorbeer streut.
He! Gebt dem Ehrenmann
sogleich . . .

MONOSTATOS
Schon deine Gnade macht mich reich!

SARASTRO
. . . nur siebenundsiebzig Sohlenstreich.

MONOSTATOS
Ach, Herr, den Lohn verhofft ich nicht!

SARASTRO
Nicht Dank, es ist ja meine
Pflicht!

(Monostatos wird abgeführt)

CHOR
Es lebe Sarastro, der göttliche Weise!
Er lohnet und strafet in ähnlichem
Kreise.

SARASTRO
Führt diese beiden Fremdlinge
In unsern Prüfungstempel ein;
Bedecket ihre Häupter dann,
Sie müssen erst gereinigt sein.

*(Sprecher und zweiter priester
bringen eine Art Sack und bedecken
die Haupter der beiden Fremden)*

CHOR
Wenn Tugend und Gerechtigkeit
Der Grossen Pfad mit Ruhm bestreut,
Dann ist die Erd' ein Himmelreich,
Und Sterbliche den Göttern gleich.

By this rare bird's cunning
he sought to steal Pamina from you.
I alone was able to catch him!
You know me! My watchfulness . . .

SARASTRO
. . . deserves a laurel wreath.
Ho there! Give this honourable
man at once . . .

MONOSTATOS
Your generosity will enrich me!

SARASTRO
. . . seventy seven strokes of the
bastinado!

MONOSTATOS
My lord, I don't deserve this reward!

SARASTRO
Do not thank me! I only do my
duty!

(Monostatos is led away)

CHORUS
Long live Sarastro, the godlike sage!
He rewards and punishes with equal
justice.

SARASTRO
Conduct these two strangers
into our temple of ordeals;
and cover their heads,
for they must first be purified.

*(The Speaker and the second priest
bring a kind of hood and cover the
heads of the two strangers)*

CHORUS
When virtue and justice spread
glory on the path of the great,
then the kingdom of Heaven will be
on earth and mortals resemble the
gods!

Zweiter Aufzug

Act two

ERSTER AUFTRITT

Ein Palmenwald. Sarastro und die Priester kommen mit feierlichen Schritten, jeder mit einem Palmenzweig in der Hand. Ein Marsch mit Blasinstrumenten begleitet den Zug

9. MARSCH DER PRIESTER

SARASTRO
(nach einer Pause)
Ihr eingeweihten Diener der Götter Isis und Osiris! Mit reiner Seele erklär ich euch, dass unsere heutige Versammlung eine der wichtigsten unserer Zeit ist: Tamino, ein Königssohn, zwanzig Jahre seines Alters, wandelt an der nördlichen Pforte unseres Tempels, will seinen nächtlichen Schleier von sich reissen und ins Heiligtum des grössten Lichtes blicken. Diesen Tugendhaften zu bewachen, ihm freundschaftlich die Hand zu bieten, ist heute unsere Pflicht.

ERSTER PRIESTER
(steht auf)
Besitzt er Tugend?

SARASTRO
Tugend!

ZWEITER PRIESTER
Auch Verschwiegenheit

SCENE 1

A palm grove. Enter Sarastro and the priests in solemn procession, each with a palm-branch in his hand. A march on wind instruments accompanies the procession

9. MARCH OF THE PRIESTS

SARASTRO
(after a pause)
Consecrated votaries of the gods Isis and Osiris! With a pure heart I declare to you that our gathering today is of the greatest moment for our time. Tamino, a king's son, twenty years of age, waits at the north gate of our temple; he wishes to tear off his dark veils and look upon the great light in the sanctuary. Our duty today is to watch over this virtuous youth and extend to him the hand of friendship.

1st PRIEST
(rising)
Is he virtuous?

SARASTRO
He is.

2nd PRIEST
Can he keep silence?

SARASTRO
Verschwiegenheit!

DRITTER PRIESTER
Ist wohltätig?

SARASTRO
Wohltätig! – Haltet ihr ihn für würdig, so
folgt meinem Beispiel . . .
(Sie blasen dreimal in die Hörner)
Sarastro dankt euch im Namen der
Menschheit. Die Götter haben Pamina,
das sanfte, tugendhafte Mädchen, dem
Jüngling bestimmt. Dies ist der Grund,
warum ich sie der Mutter entriss. Dieses
Weib dünkt sich gross, hofft durch
Blendwerk und Aberglauben das Volk zu
berücken und unsern festen Tempelbau zu
zerstören. Das soll sie nicht! Tamino
selbst soll ihn mit uns
befestigen.

*(Der dreimalige Akkord mit den
Hörnern wird von allen wiederholt)*

SPRECHER
Grosser Sarastro, wird Tamino auch die
harten Prüfungen, die seiner warten,
bestehen? Bedenke: Er ist ein Prinz.

SARASTRO
Mehr! Er ist ein Mensch!

SPRECHER
Wenn er nun aber in seiner frühen
Jugend leblos erblasste?

SARASTRO
Dann ist er Osiris und Isis gegeben
und wird der Götter Freuden früher
fühlen als wir.
(Dreimaliger Akkord wird wiederholt)
Man führe Tamino mit seinem
Reisegefährten in den Vorhof des
Tempels ein.
*(Zum Sprecher, der vor ihm
niederkniet)*
Und du vollziehe dein heiliges Amt: Lehre
sie die Macht der Götter
erkennen!

SARASTRO
He can.

3rd PRIEST
Is he benevolent?

SARASTRO
He is. If you deem him worthy,
follow my example . . .
(They blow their horns three times)
Sarastro thanks you in the name of
humanity. The gods have destined
the gentle, virtuous maid Pamina for
this youth: it was for this that I
took her from her mother, a woman
who vaunts herself and hopes to
delude the people by trickery and
superstition and to destroy the firm
foundation of our temple. It shall
not be! Tamino himself shall help
us strengthen it.

*(The threefold chord on the horns
is repeated)*

SPEAKER
Great Sarastro, can Tamino endure
the severe ordeals that await him?
Consider: he is a prince.

SARASTRO
More! He is a man!

SPEAKER
But what if, in his early youth,
he now pales in death?

SARASTRO
Then he is given over to Osiris
and Isis and will experience the
joys of heaven sooner than we.
(The threefold chord is repeated)
Let Tamino and his travelling
companion be led into the forecourt
of the temple.
*(To the Speaker, who kneels before
him)*
And you, discharge your sacred
duty: teach them to recognise the
power of the gods!

10. ARIE MIT CHOR

SARASTRO
O, Isis und Osiris, schenket
Der Weisheit Geist dem neuen Paar!
Die ihr den Schritt der Wand'rer lenket,
Stärkt mit Geduld sie in Gefahr.

CHOR
Stärkt mit Geduld sie in Gefahr.

SARASTRO
Lasst sie der Prüfung Früchte sehen;
Doch sollten sie zu Grabe gehen,
So lohnt der Tugend kühnen Lauf,
Nehmt sie in euren Wohnsitz auf.

CHOR
Nehmt sie in euren Wohnsitz auf.

*(Sarastro geht voraus, dann alle ihm
nach ab)*

ZWEITER AUFTRITT

*Kurzer Vorhof des Tempels. Nacht.
Tamino und Papageno werden von drei
Priestern hereingefuhrt. Sie losen ihnen
die Sacke ab; die Priester gehen dann ab.*

TAMINO
Eine schreckliche Nacht! Papageno, bist
du noch bei mir?

PAPAGENO
Ja freilich!

TAMINO
Wo denkst du, dass wir uns befinden?

PAPAGENO
Wo? wenn's nicht finster wäre, wollt ich
dir's schon sagen, aber so . . .
(Donnerschlag) O weh!

TAMINO
Was ist's?

10. ARIA WITH CHORUS

SARASTRO
O Isis and Osiris, bestow
the spirit of wisdom on this new
pair! You who direct travellers'
steps, strengthen them with
patience in danger.

CHORUS
Strengthen them with patience in
danger.

SARASTRO
Let them see the fruits of their trial;
yet should they succumb and perish
reward their virtue's bold enterprise
and receive them in your blessed
abode.

CHORUS
Receive them in your blessed abode.

*(Exit Sarastro, followed by all the
others)*

SCENE 2

*Small forecourt of the temple. Night.
Tamino and Papageno are led in by
three priests, who take off their
hoods and then go out.*

TAMINO
It's dreadfully dark! Papageno, are
you still there?

PAPAGENO
Of course I am.

TAMINO
Where do you think we are?

PAPAGENO
Where? Well, if it weren't so dark I
might be able to tell you, but . . .
(thunder) Oh dear!

TAMINO
What is it?

PAPAGENO
Mir wird wohl bei der Sache!

TAMINO
Du hast Furcht, wie ich höre.

PAPAGENO
Furcht eben nicht, nur eiskalt läuft's mir über den Rücken. *(Starker Donnerschlag)* O weh!

PAPAGENO
I don't like this.

TAMINO
You're afraid, I can tell.

PAPAGENO
Not exactly afraid, but cold shivers are running down my spine. *(Louder thunder)* Oh, oh!

DRITTER AUFTRITT

Priester mit Fackeln, die Vorigen

SPRECHER
Ihr Fremdlinge, was treibt euch an, in unsere Mauern zu dringen?

TAMINO
Freundschaft und Liebe.

SPRECHER
Bist du bereit, sie mit deinem Leben zu erkämpfen?

TAMINO
Ja!

SPRECHER
Auch wenn der Tod dein Los wäre?

TAMINO
Ja!

SPRECHER
Prinz! Noch ist's Zeit zu weichen — einen Schritt weiter, und es ist zu spät.

TAMINO
Weisheitslehre sei mein Sieg; Pamina, das holde Mädchen, mein Lohn.

SPRECHER
Du unterziehst jeder Prüfung dich?

TAMINO
Jeder!

SCENE 3

Enter priests with torches

SPEAKER
Strangers, what has led you to enter within our walls?

TAMINO
Friendship and love.

SPEAKER
Are you prepared to fight for them with your life?

TAMINO
Yes!

SPEAKER
Even if death were your lot?

TAMINO
Yes!

SPEAKER
Prince, there is still time to turn back. One step further and it will be too late.

TAMINO
Let the knowledge of wisdom be my goal and the lovely Pamina my reward.

SPEAKER
You will submit to every ordeal?

TAMINO
Every one!

SPRECHER
Reiche mir deine Hand! So!

SPEAKER
Give me your hand! There!

ZWEITER PRIESTER
Willst auch du die Weisheitsliebe erkämpfen,
Papageno?

2nd PRIEST
Papageno, will you too fight for the
love of wisdom?

PAPAGENO
Kämpfen ist meine Sache nicht. Ich
verlange auch im Grunde gar keine
Weisheit. Ich bin so ein Naturmensch,
der sich mit Schlaf, Speise und Trank
begnügt; und wenn es ja sein könnte,
das ich mir einmal ein schönes Weibchen
fange . . .

PAPAGENO
Fighting's not my line. And I don't
really and truly yearn for wisdom.
I'm just a simple man: sleep, food
and drink are quite enough for me,
though if I could possibly get
myself a pretty little
wife . . .

ZWEITER PRIESTER
Die wirst du nie erhalten, wenn du dich
nicht unseren Prüfungen unterziehst.

2nd PRIEST
That you'll never obtain unless you
undergo our tests.

PAPAGENO
Worin besteht diese Prüfung?

PAPAGENO
What do they consist of?

ZWEITER PRIESTER
Dich allen unseren Gesetzen zu
unterwerfen, selbst den Tod nicht zu
scheuen.

2nd PRIEST
To submit to all our rules, and not
even to shrink from
death.

PAPAGENO
Ich bleibe ledig!

PAPAGENO
I'll stay single!

ZWEITER PRIESTER
Wenn nun aber Sarastro dir ein Mädchen
aufbewahrt hätte, das an Farbe und
Kleidung dir ganz gleich wäre?

2nd PRIEST
But if Sarastro had kept for you a
maid just like you in colour and
dress?

PAPAGENO
Mir gleich? Ist sie jung?

PAPAGENO
Like me? Is she young?

ZWEITER PRIESTER
Jung und schön!

2nd PRIEST
Young and beautiful!

PAPAGENO
Und heisst?

PAPAGENO
What's her name?

ZWEITER PRIESTER
Papagena

2nd PRIEST
Papagena

PAPAGENO
Wie? Pa . . . ?

PAPAGENO
What? Pa . . . ?

ZWEITER PRIESTER
Papagena.

PAPAGENO
Papagena? – Die mocht ich aus blosser
Neugierde sehen.

ZWEITER PRIESTER
Sehen kannst du sie!

PAPAGENO
Aber wenn ich sie gesehen habe, muss ich
sterben? Ich bleibe ledig!

ZWEITER PRIESTER
Sehen kannst du sie. Aber wirst du so viel
Standhaftigkeit besitzen, kein Wort mit ihr
zu sprechen?

PAPAGENO
O ja!

ZWEITER PRIESTER
Deine Hand! Du sollst sie sehen.

SPRECHER
Auch dir, Prinz, legen die Götter
Stillschweigen auf. Du wirst Pamina
sehen, aber sie nie sprechen dürfen! Dies
ist der Anfang eurer Prüfungszeit.

11. DUETT

SPRECHER und ZWEITER PRIESTER
Bewahret euch vor Weibertücken:
Dies ist des Bundes erste Pflicht!
Manch weiser Mann liess sich berücken,
Er fehlte und versah sich's nicht.
Verlassen sah er sich am Ende,
Vergolten seine Treu mit Hohn!
Vergebens rang er seine Hände,
Tod und Verzweiflung war sein Lohn.

(Priester ab)

VIERTER AUFTRITT

Papageno, Tamino

2nd PRIEST
Papagena.

PAPAGENO
Papagena? – I'd like to see her out
of sheer curiosity.

2nd PRIEST
You may see her.

PAPAGENO
But when I've seen her, have I got to
die? I'll stay single!

2nd PRIEST
You may see her. But will you have
enough strength of mind not to
speak a word to her?

PAPAGENO
Oh yes!

2nd PRIEST
Your hand on it! You shall see her.

SPEAKER
On you too, prince, the gods
enjoin silence. You shall see Pamina,
but must not speak to her! This is
the beginning of your probation.

11. DUET

SPEAKER and 2nd PRIEST
Beware the wiles of women:
this is the first duty of your bond!
Many a wise man has let himself be
misled, succumbed and been caught
off guard. At last he has found himself abandoned, his faith requited
with mockery. In vain he has wrung
his hands; death and despair were
his lot.

(Exeunt priests)

SCENE 4

Papageno, Tamino

PAPAGENO
He, Lichter her! Lichter her! Das ist doch
wunderlich: so oft einen die Herren
verlassen, sieht man mit offenen Augen
nichts mehr!

PAPAGENO
Ho there, lights! Bring lights! It's
very strange: as soon as these
gentlemen leave us, we can see
nothing even with our eyes open!

TAMINO
Ertrag es mit Geduld und denke, es ist der
Götter Wille.

TAMINO
Bear it with patience, and remember
it is the will of the gods.

FÜNFTER AUFTRITT

*Die drei Damen (aus der Versenkung), die
Vorigen*

SCENE 5

*The three ladies appear through a
trapdoor*

12. QUINTETT

12. QUINTET

DIE DREI DAMEN
Wie? Wie? Wie?
Ihr an diesem Schreckensort?
Nie, nie, nie
Kommt ihr glücklich wieder fort!
Tamino, dir ist Tod geschworen!
Du, Papageno, bist verloren!

THE THREE LADIES
What? What is this?
You here in this fearful place?
Never, nevermore
will you emerge to happiness!
Tamino, you are doomed to death!
You, Papageno, are lost!

PAPAGENO
Nein, nein, nein! Das wär zu
viel!

PAPAGENO
No, no, no! That would be too
much.

TAMINO
Papageno, schweige still!
Willst du dein Gelübde brechen,
Nichts mit Weibern hier zu sprechen?

TAMINO
Papageno, keep quiet!
Will you break your vow here
not to speak to women?

PAPAGENO
Du hörst ja, wir sind beide hin.

PAPAGENO
But you heard, we are both done
for!

TAMINO
Stille, sag ich! Schweige still!

TAMINO
Quiet, I say! Hold your tongue!

PAPAGENO
Immer still und immer still!

PAPAGENO
Always quiet, always hush!

DIE DREI DAMEN
Ganz nah ist euch die Königin!
Sie drang im Tempel heimlich ein.

THE THREE LADIES
The Queen is very near to you!
She has secretly entered the temple.

PAPAGENO
Wie? Was? Sie soll im Tempel sein?

PAPAGENO
What? She is in the temple?

67

TAMINO
Stille, sag ich! Schweige still!
Wirst du immer so vermessen
Deiner Eidespflicht vergessen?

TAMINO
Quiet, I say! Hold your tongue!
Are you always so bold
as to forget a solemn oath?

DIE DREI DAMEN
Tamino, hör! Du bist verloren!
Gedenke an die Königin!
Man zischelt viel sich in die Ohren
Von dieser Priester falschem Sinn.

THE THREE LADIES
Tamino, listen! You are lost!
Think of the Queen!
Rumour is rife
about the priests' falsity.

TAMINO
(für sich)
Ein Weiser prüft und achtet nicht,
Was der gemeine Pöbel spricht.

TAMINO
(to himself)
A wise man observes, and pays no
heed to the gossip of the common
crowd.

DIE DREI DAMEN
Man sagt, wer ihrem Bunde schwört,
Der fährt zur Höll' mit Haut und
Haar.

THE THREE LADIES
It's said that whoever joins their
number is damned, body and soul,
to Hell.

PAPAGENO
Das wär beim Teufel unerhört!
Sag an, Tamino, ist das wahr?

PAPAGENO
The devil! This is unheard-of!
Tell me, Tamino, is it true?

TAMINO
Geschwätz, von Weibern nachgesagt,
Von Heuchlern aber ausgedacht.

TAMINO
Gossip repeated by old wives
but inspired by hypocrites.

PAPAGENO
Doch sagt es auch die Königin.

PAPAGENO
But the Queen says so too.

TAMINO
Sie ist ein Weib, hat Weibersinn.
Sei still, mein Wort sei dir genug,
Denk deiner Pflicht und handle klug.

TAMINO
She is a woman, with a woman's
mind. Keep quiet; my word should
be enough; think of your duty and
act prudently.

DIE DREI DAMEN
(zu Tamino)
Warum bist du mit uns so spröde?

THE THREE LADIES
(to Tamino)
Why are you so reserved with us?

*Tamino deutet an, dass oer nicht sprechen
darf*

*Tamino indicates that he may not
speak*

DIE DREI DAMEN
Auch Papageno schweigt – so rede!

THE THREE LADIES
And Papageno's silent – speak!

PAPAGENO
(heimlich zu den Damen)
Ich möchte gerne ... woll ...

TAMINO
Still!

PAPAGENO
Ihr seht, dass ich nicht soll ...

TAMINO
Still!

PAPAGENO
Dass ich nicht kann das Plaudern lassen,
Ist wahrlich eine Schand für mich!

TAMINO
Dass du nicht kannst das Plaudern lassen,
Ist wahrlich eine Schand für mich!

DIE DREI DAMEN
Wir müssen sie mit Scham verlassen,
Es plaudert keiner sicherlich.

TAMINO, PAPAGENO
Sie müssen uns mit Scham verlassen,
Es plaudert keiner sicherlich.

ALLE
Von festem Geiste ist ein Mann;
Er denket, was er sprechen kann.

PRIESTER
(von innen)
Entweiht ist die heilige Schwelle!
Hinab mit den Weibern zur Hölle!

DIE DREI DAMEN
O weh!

*(Die Damen stürzen in die
Versenkung)*

PAPAGENO
O weh!

(Er fällt zu Boden)

PAPAGENO
(secretly to the ladies)
I'd be glad to ... but ...

TAMINO
Silence!

PAPAGENO
You see, I may not ...

TAMINO
Silence!

PAPAGENO
That I can't hold my tongue
is truly a disgrace to me.

TAMINO
That you can't hold your tongue
is indeed a disgrace to you.

THE THREE LADIES
We must leave you with shame,
for neither of you will speak.

TAMINO, PAPAGENO
You must leave us with shame,
for neither of us indeed will speak.

ALL
A man is strong in spirit:
he thinks before he speaks.

PRIESTS
(from within)
Our sacred threshold is profaned!
To Hell with these women!

THE THREE LADIES
Alas!

*(They disappear through the trap-
door)*

PAPAGENO
Alas!

(He falls to the ground)

*Sprecher und zweiter Priester mit Fackeln,
Tamino, Papageno*

SPRECHER
Tamino! Dein standhaft männliches
Betragen hat gesiegt. Aber du hast noch
manch rauhen und gefährlichen Weg zu
wandern! So komm!

(ab)

ZWEITER PRIESTER
Steh auf, Papageno!

PAPAGENO
Ich lieg in einer Ohnmacht!

ZWEITER PRIESTER
Auf! Sei ein Mann!

PAPAGENO
Aber wenn mir die Götter eine Papagena
bestimmten, warum muss ich sie denn mit
so viel Gefahren
erringen?

ZWEITER PRIESTER
Komm! Ich führe dich weiter!

VERWANDLUNG

*Ein Garten, worin Pamina schläft. Der
Mond beleuchtet ihr Gesicht.*

SIEBENTER AUFTRITT

Monostatos, Pamina

13.   ARIE

MONOSTATOS
(nähert sich Pamina)
Alles fühlt der Liebe Freuden,
Schnäbelt, tändelt, herzt und küsst;
Und ich soll die Liebe meiden,
Weil ein Schwarzer hässlich ist.
Ist mir denn kein Herz gegeben?
Bin ich nicht von Fleisch und Blut?

SCENE 6

*Speaker and 2nd priest with torches,
Tamino, Papageno*

SPEAKER
Tamino! Your steadfast, manly
behaviour has triumphed. But you
still have many a rough and
perilous path to tread! Come then!

(Exit with Tamino)

2nd PRIEST
Stand up, Papageno!

PAPAGENO
I've fainted!

2nd PRIEST
Get up! Be a man!

PAPAGENO
But if the gods have arranged a
Papagena for me, why do I have to
go through so many dangers to get
her?

2nd PRIEST
Come on! I'll lead the way!

TRANSFORMATION

*A garden, in which Pamina is asleep.
The moonlight shines on her face.*

SCENE 7

Monostatos, Pamina

13.   ARIA

MONOSTATOS
(coming close to Pamina)
All men feel love's rapture,
bill and coo, caress and kiss;
and I must deny myself love
because of my ugly black face.
Has no heart then been given me?
Am I not of flesh and blood?

Immer ohne Weibchen leben,	Always to live without a wife
Wäre wahrlich Höllenglut!	would be hell indeed!

Drum so will ich, weil ich lebe,	Therefore, since I am living,
Schnäbeln, küssen, zärtlich sein!	I'll toy and kiss and fondle!
Lieber guter Mond, vergebe,	Dear good moon, forgive me,
Eine Weisse nahm mich ein.	her whiteness has captured me.
Weiss ist schön! Ich muss sie küssen;	White is fair! I must kiss her;
Mond, verstecke dich dazu!	moon, hide your face!
Sollt es dich zu sehr verdriessen,	If it should shock you too much,
Oh, so mach die Augen zu!	then close your eyes!

(Er schleicht langsam und leise zu Pamina hin) — *(He steals slowly and quietly towards Pamina)*

ACHTER AUFTRITT — SCENE 8

Die Königin kommt unter Donner aus der Versenkung — *The Queen appears through a trapdoor to the sound of thunder*

KÖNIGIN
Zurück!

QUEEN
Stand back!

PAMINA
(erwacht)
Ihr Götter!

PAMINA
(waking)
Ye gods!

MONOSTATOS
O weh! Das ist die Königin der Nacht.

MONOSTATOS
Woe is me! That is the Queen of Night!

PAMINA
Meine Mutter!

PAMINA
My mother!

(Sie fällt ihr die Arme) — *(She falls into her arms)*

MONOSTATOS
Mutter? Das muss man belauschen.

MONOSTATOS
Her mother! I must hear this.

(Schleicht ab) — *(slinks away)*

KÖNIGIN
Wo ist der Jüngling, den ich an dich sandte?

QUEEN
Where is the youth I sent to you?

PAMINA
Er hat sich den Eingeweihten gewidment.

PAMINA
He has dedicated himself to the initiates.

KÖNIGIN
Nun bist du auf ewig mir entrissen.

QUEEN
Then you are lost to me for ever.

71

PAMINA
O fliehen wir, liebe Mutter! Unter
deinem Schutze trotze ich jeder Gefahr.

KÖNIGIN
Schutz? Mit deines Vaters Tod ging meine
Macht zu Grabe. Er übergab freiwillig den
siebenfachen Sonnenkreis den
Eingeweihten — diesen mächtigen
Sonnenkreis trägt Sarastro auf der
Brust.

PAMINA
So ist wohl auch der fremde Jüngling auf
immer für mich verloren?

KÖNIGIN
Siehst du hier diesen Stahl? Er ist für Sarastro geschliffen — du wirst ihn tödten,
und den mächtigen Sonnenkreis mir
überliefern.

PAMINA
Aber, teure Mutter!

14. ARIE

KÖNIGIN
Der Hölle Rache kocht in meinem Herzen,
Tod und Verzweiflung flammet um mich
her!
Fühlt nicht durch dich Sarastro
Todesschmerzen.
So bist du meine Tochter nimmermehr.
Verstossen sei auf ewig, verlassen sei auf
ewig.
Zertrümmert sei'n auf ewig alle Bande der
Natur,
Wenn nicht durch dich Sarastro wird
erblassen!
Hort, Rachegötter! Hört der Mutter
Schwur!

(Sie versinkt)

NEUNTER AUFTRITT

PAMINA
Morden soll ich? Das kann ich nicht!

PAMINA
O let us fly, mother dear! Under
your protection I'll defy any danger.

QUEEN
Protection? With your father's death
my power came to an end. He
freely surrendered the sevenfold
shield of the sun to the initiates —
that mighty shield of the sun that
Sarastro wears on his breast.

PAMINA
Then is the young stranger lost to
me forever too?

QUEEN
Do you see this blade? It was
forged for Sarastro. You shall kill
him, and bring me the mighty
shield of the sun.

PAMINA
But dear mother!

14. ARIA

QUEEN
The vengeance of Hell rages in my
heart, death and despair burn all
around me!
If Sarastro does not through you
suffer death's torments, nevermore
be my daughter.
Be repudiated, disowned for ever,
all nature's bonds be for ever
severed,
if Sarastro does not through you
meet his end!
Hear, ye gods of vengeance! Hear a
mother's vow!

(She sinks into the earth)

SCENE 9

PAMINA
Must I kill him? I cannot do it!

ZEHNTER AUFTRITT	SCENE 10

Pamina mit dem Dolch in der Hand, Monostatos kommt schnell, heimlich und sehr freudig

Pamina, the dagger in her hand. Monostatos enters quickly, stealthily and joyfully

PAMINA
Was soll ich tun?

PAMINA
What can I do?

MONOSTATOS
Dich mir anvertrauen!

MONOSTATOS
Trust yourself to me!

(nimmt ihr den Dolch weg)

(takes the dagger from her)

PAMINA
Dir!?

PAMINA
To you?!

MONOSTATOS
Du hast also nur einen Weg, Dich und deine Mutter zu retten.

MONOSTATOS
There is only one way now for you to save yourself and your mother.

PAMINA
Der wäre?

PAMINA
And what is that?

MONOSTATOS
Mich zu lieben!

MONOSTATOS
By loving me.

PAMINA
Götter!

PAMINA
Ye gods!

MONOSTATOS
Nun, Mädchen! Ja oder nein?

MONOSTATOS
Well, girl, yes or no?

PAMINA
Nein!

PAMINA
No!

ELFTER AUFTRITT	SCENE 11

MONOSTATOS
So fahre denn hin!

MONOSTATOS
Then die!

(Sarastro tritt hervor und hält ihn zurück)

(Sarastro has entered and restrains him)

MONOSTATOS
Herr, ich bin unschuldig! Ich wollte dich rächen.

MONOSTATOS
Lord, I am innocent! I intended to avenge you.

SARASTRO
Ich weiss nur allzuviel – weiss dass deine
Seele eben so schwarz als dein Gesicht ist.
Geh!

MONOSTATOS
(im Abgehen)
Jetzt such ich die Mutter auf,
weil die Tochter mir nicht beschieden
ist.

(ab)

ZWÖLFTER AUFTRITT

Pamina, Sarastro

PAMINA
Herr! Strafe meine Mutter nicht, der
Schmerz, mich zu verlieren . . .

SARASTRO
Ich weiss alles. Weiss, dass sie in
unterirdischen Gemächern des Tempels
herumirrt und Rache über mich und die
Menschheit kocht. Du sollst sehen, wie
ich mich an deiner Mutter
räche.

15. ARIE

SARASTRO
In diesen heil'gen Hallen
Kennt man die Rache nicht,
Und ist ein Mensch gefallen,
Führt Liebe ihn zur Pflicht.
Dann wandelt er an Freundes Hand
Vergnügt und froh ins bess're Land.
In diesen heil'gen Mauern,
Wo Mensch den Menschen liebt,
Kann kein Verräter lauern,
Weil man dem Feind vergibt.
Wen solche Lehren nicht erfreun,
Verdienet nicht, ein Mensch zu sein.

VERWANDLUNG

Ein Halle

SARASTRO
I know only too much. Your soul is
as black as your face.
Go!

MONOSTATOS
(as he goes)
Now I must seek out the mother,
since the daughter isn't meant
for me.

(exit)

SCENE 12

Pamina, Sarastro

PAMINA
Lord, do not punish my mother!
The grief of losing me . . .

SARASTRO
I know everything. I know that she
is wandering about in the
subterranean vaults of the temple
and preparing vengeance on me and
all mankind. You shall see what
revenge I will take on your mother.

15. ARIA

SARASTRO
Within these sacred halls
vengeance is unknown,
and if a man falls from grace
love leads him back to his duty.
Then, guided by a friendly hand,
he contentedly enters a better land.
Within this holy masonry,
where men love their fellows,
no traitor can lurk,
for we forgive our foes.
He who cannot profit by this
teaching is not worthy to be a man.

TRANSFORMATION

A hall

DREIZEHNTER AUFTRITT

Tamino und Papageno werden von zwei Priestern hereingeführt.

SPRECHER
Hier seid ihr euch beide allein überlassen. Sobald die Posaune tont, dann nehmt ihr euren Weg dahin. Vergesst das Wort nicht: Schweigen.

ZWEITER PRIESTER
Papageno, wer an diesem Orte sein Stillschweigen bricht, den strafen die Götter durch Donner und Blitz. Leb wohl!

(Die Priester entfernen sich)

VIERZEHNTER AUFTRITT

Papageno, Tamino

PAPAGENO
(nach einer Pause)
Tamino!

TAMINO
(verweisend)
St!

PAPAGENO
Das ist ein lustiges Leben! Wär ich doch in meiner Strohhütte, oder im Wald, so hört' ich doch manchmal einen Vogel pfeifen!

TAMINO
St!

PAPAGENO
Mit mir selbst werd ich wohl sprechen dürfen.

TAMINO
St!

SCENE 13

Tamino and Papageno are led in by two priests

SPEAKER
You are to remain here alone. As soon as the trumpets sound, proceed that way. Do not forget your instructions: silence.

2nd PRIEST
Papageno, anyone breaking silence in this place is punished by the gods with thunder and lightening. Farewell!

(Exeunt priests)

SCENE 14

Papageno, Tamino

PAPAGENO
(after a pause)
Tamino!

TAMINO
(rebuking him)
Sh!

PAPAGENO
What a gay life! Were I in my straw hut, or in the woods, at least I'd sometimes hear a bird singing!

TAMINO
Sh!

PAPAGENO
Aren't I allowed to talk to myself?

TAMINO
Sh!

PAPAGENO
(singt)
La la la — la la la!
Nicht einmal einen Tropfen Wasser
bekommt man bei diesen Leuten, viel
weniger sonst was.

FÜNFZEHNTER AUFTRITT

*Ein altes, hassliches Weib kommt aus der
Versenkung und halt einen grossen
Becher mit Wasser. Die Vorigen.*

PAPAGENO
He, du Alte! Ist dieser Becher für mich?

WEIB
Ja, mein Engel!

PAPAGENO
(trinkt)
Wasser!

WEIB
Freilich, mein Engel!

PAPAGENO
So, so! Geh, Alte, setz dich
her zu mir, mir ist die Zeit
verdammt lang. Wie alt bist
du dann?

WEIB
Achtzehn Jahr und zwei Minuten.

PAPAGENO
Achtzehn Jahr und zwei Minuten?

WEIB
Ja!

PAPAGENO
Haha! Ei, du junger Engel! Hast du auch
einen Geliebten?

WEIB
Freilich!

PAPAGENO
Ist er auch so jung wie du?

PAPAGENO
(singing)
La la la — la la la!
These people won't even give us a
drop of water, let alone anything
else.

SCENE 15

*An ugly old woman appears through
a trapdoor, holding a large tumbler
of water.*

PAPAGENO
Hey, granny! Is this for me?

WOMAN
Yes, my love.

PAPAGENO
(drinking)
Water!

WOMAN
Yes indeed, my love.

PAPAGENO
Well, well! Come and sit here
beside me, granny: time's passing
confoundedly slowly for me. How
old are you?

WOMAN
Eighteen years and two minutes.

PAPAGENO
Eighteen years and two minutes?

WOMAN
That's right.

PAPAGENO
Ha, ha! Well, my young angel, have
you a sweetheart?

WOMAN
Of course!

PAPAGENO
Is he as young as you?

WEIB
Nicht gar, er ist um zehn Jahre älter.

PAPAGENO
Um zehn Jahre ist er älter als du? Das
muss eine Liebe sein! Wie nennt sich
dein Liebhaber?

WEIB
Papageno.

PAPAGENO
(erschrickt; pause)
Papageno? Wo ist der denn, dieser
Papageno?

WEIB
Da sitzt er, mein Engel!

PAPAGENO
Ich wär dein Geliebter?

WEIB
Ja, mein Engel!

PAPAGENO
Sag mir, wie du heisst?

WEIB
Ich heiss' . . .

(Donner. Die Alte hinkt schnell ab)

PAPAGENO
Weg ist sie! Nun sprech ich kein Wort
mehr!

SECHZEHNTER AUFTRITT

*Die drei Knaben: der eine hat die Flöte,
der andere das Glockenspiel. Ein schön
gedeckter Tisch erscheint. Die
Vorigen.*

16. TERZETT

DIE DREI KNABEN
Seid uns zum zweitenmal willkommen,
Ihr Männer, in Sarastros Reich.

WOMAN
Not quite; he's about ten years older.

PAPAGENO
About ten years older than you?
This must be quite a love affair!
And what's your sweetheart's name?

WOMAN
Papageno

PAPAGENO
(startled, after a pause)
Papageno? Where is he then, this
Papageno?

WOMAN
Why, there he sits, my love!

PAPAGENO
I'm your sweetheart?

WOMAN
Yes, dearest!

PAPAGENO
Tell me, what's your name?

WOMAN
My name is . . .

(Thunder. She hobbles off quickly)

PAPAGENO
She's gone! I won't say another
word!

SCENE 16

*Enter the three boys: one carries
the flute, another the chime of bells.
A table laden with food and drink
appears.*

16. TRIO

THE THREE BOYS
Welcome a second time,
strangers, to Sarastro's realm.

Er schickt, was man euch abgenommen,
Die Flöte und die Glöckchen euch.
Wollt ihr die Speisen nicht verschmähen,
So esset, trinket froh davon.
Wenn wir zum drittenmal uns sehen,
Ist Freude eures Mutes Lohn!
Tamino, Mut! Nah ist das Ziel.
Du, Papageno, schweige still!

(Sie gehen ab)

SIEBZEHNTER AUFTRITT

Papageno, Tamino

PAPAGENO
Tamino, wollen wir nicht speisen?

Tamino bläst auf seiner Flöte

PAPAGENO
Blase du nur fort auf deiner Flöte! Ich
will schon schweigen, wenn ich immer
solch gute Bissen bekomme. Ob auch
der Keller so gut bestellt ist? Ah! Ein
Götterwein!

ACHTZEHNTER AUFTRITT

Pamina, die Vorigen

PAMINA
(freudig)
Du hier, Tamino? Ich hörte deine Flöte
und lief dem Tone nach. Aber du bist
traurig? Sprichst nicht eine Silbe mit
deiner Pamina?

Tamino seufzt und winkt ihr fortzugehen

PAMINA
Wie? Ich soll dich meiden? Liebst du mich
nicht mehr? Papageno, sage du mir,
sag . . .

*Papageno (hat einen Brocken im Munde,
winkt fortzugehen)*

He sends you back the flute and
bells which had been taken from
you. If you will accept this meal,
eat and drink in good cheer.
When we meet for the third time
your courage will be rewarded with
joy! Courage, Tamino! The goal is
near. Papageno, keep silent!

(Exeunt)

SCENE 17

Papageno, Tamino

PAPAGENO
Tamino, can't we eat?

Tamino plays his flute

PAPAGENO
All right, you play your flute! I can
keep quiet if only I'm given such
good things to eat. Is the wine-
cellar as well stocked? Ah!
heavenly wine!

SCENE 18

Enter Pamina

PAMINA
(joyfully)
You here, Tamino? I heard your
flute and ran towards the sound.
But you are sad — have you not a
word for your Pamina?

Tamino sighs and motions her away

PAMINA
What? I am to go away? Don't you
love me any more? Papageno, you
tell me . . .

*Papageno (his mouth full, signs to
her to go away)*

PAMINA
Wie? Auch du? Liebster, einziger
Tamino! Oh, das ist mehr als Tod!

17. ARIE

PAMINA
Ach, ich fühl's es ist verschwunden,
Ewig hin der Liebe Glück!
Nimmer kommt ihr, Wonnestunden,
Meinem Herzen mehr zurück!
Sieh, Tamino, diese Tränen
Fliessen, Trauter, dir allein.
Fühlst du nicht der Liebe Sehnen,
So wird Ruh im Tode sein!

(ab)

VERWANDLUNG

*Das Theater verwandelt sich in das
Gewölbe von Pyramiden*

NEUNZEHNTER AUFTRITT

Sarastro, Priester

18. CHOR DER PRIESTER

O, Isis und Osiris, welche Wonne!
Die düstre Nacht verscheucht der Glanz
der Sonne,
Bald fühlt der edle Jüngling neues Leben;
Bald ist er unserm Dienste ganz ergeben.
Sein Geist ist kühn, sein Herz ist rein,
Bald wird er unser würdig sein.

ZWANZIGSTER AUFTRITT

*Die Vorigen. Tamino von einem Priester
geführt. Später Pamina.*

SARASTRO
Tamino, dein Betragen war bisher
männlich und gelassen; nun hast du noch
zwei gefährliche Wege zu wandern. Mögen
die Götter dich begleiten. – Man bringe
Pamina! – Deine Hand.

PAMINA
What? You too? Tamino, my only
love! Oh, this is worse than death!

17. ARIA

PAMINA
Ah, I know it, fled for ever
is love's happiness!
Nevermore will you return
to my heart, hours of bliss!
See, Tamino, these tears
flowing for you alone, beloved.
If you do not feel love's yearning
I will seek peace in death!

(exit)

TRANSFORMATION

*A vault inside a
pyramid*

SCENE 19

Sarastro and Priests

18. CHORUS OF PRIESTS

O, Isis and Osiris, what rapture!
The sun's rays have banished the
darkness of night;
soon the noble youth will feel new life,
soon he will be fully sworn into our
service. His spirit is brave, his heart is
pure; soon he will be worthy of us.

SCENE 20

*Tamino is led in by a priest. Later
Pamina.*

SARASTRO
Tamino, so far your bearing has
been manly and composed: now
you have two further perilous paths
to tread. May the gods go with you.
– Bring in Pamina! – Give me your
hand.

(Pamina wird hereingeführt; Sarastro löst die Bande am Sacke auf)

PAMINA
Wo bin ich? Wo ist Tamino?

SARASTRO
Er wartet deiner, um dir das letzte Lebewohl zu sagen.

PAMINA
Das letzte Lebewohl! Wo ist er?

SARASTRO
Hier!

PAMINA
Tamino!

TAMINO
Zurück!

19. TERZETT

PAMINA
Soll ich dich, Teurer, nicht mehr sehn?

SARASTRO
Ihr werdet froh euch wieder sehn.

PAMINA
Dein warten tödliche Gefahren!

TAMINO
Die Götter mögen mich bewahren!

SARASTRO
Die Götter mögen ihn bewahren!

PAMINA
Du wirst dem Tode nicht entgehen;
Mir flüstert dieses Ahnung ein.

TAMINO, SARASTRO
Der Götter Wille mag geschehen,
Ihr Wink soll mir (ihm) Gesetze sein.

PAMINA
O liebtest du, wie ich dich liebe,
Du würdest nicht so ruhig sein.

(Pamina is brought in, veiled; Sarastro unties her hood)

PAMINA
Where am I? Where is Tamino?

SARASTRO
He waits to take a last farewell of you.

PAMINA
A last farewell? Where is he?

SARASTRO
Here!

PAMINA
Tamino!

TAMINO
Stand back!

19. TRIO

PAMINA
Beloved, must I never see you again?

SARASTRO
You will meet again in joy.

PAMINA
Deadly perils await you!

TAMINO
The gods will protect me!

SARASTRO
May the gods protect him!

PAMINA
You will not escape death:
I have a presentiment.

TAMINO, SARASTRO
The will of the gods must prevail;
their behest shall be my (his) law.

PAMINA
O if you loved me as I love you
you would not be so calm.

SARASTRO
Glaub mir, er fühlet gleiche Triebe,
Wird ewig dein Getreuer sein.

TAMINO
Glaub mir, ich fühle gleiche Triebe,
Werd ewig dein Getreuer sein!

SARASTRO
Die Stunde schlägt, nun müsst ihr
scheiden.

TAMINO, PAMINA
Wie bitter sind der Trennung Leiden!

SARASTRO
Tamino muss nun wieder fort.

TAMINO
Pamina, ich muss wirklich fort!

PAMINA
Tamino muss nun wirklich fort!

SARASTRO
Nun muss er fort!

TAMINO
Nun muss ich fort.

PAMINA
So musst du fort!

TAMINO
Pamina, lebe wohl!

PAMINA
Tamino, lebe wohl!

SARASTRO
Nun eile fort. Dich ruft dein Wort.
Die Stunde schlägt, wir sehn uns
wieder.

TAMINO, PAMINA
Ach, goldne Ruhe, kehre wieder!
Lebe wohl, lebe wohl!

(entfernen sich)

SARASTRO
Believe me, he shares your feelings
and will always be faithful to you.

TAMINO
Believe me, I share your feelings
and will always be faithful to you.

SARASTRO
The hour is come for you to
part.

TAMINO, PAMINA
How bitter is the pain of parting!

SARASTRO
Tamino must go now.

TAMINO
Pamina, I must indeed be gone!

PAMINA
Tamino must indeed be gone!

SARASTRO
He must be gone.

TAMINO
I must be gone.

PAMINA
You must be gone.

TAMINO
Pamina, farewell!

PAMINA
Tamino, farewell!

SARASTRO
Now haste away: your honour
summons you. The hour is come;
we'll meet again.

TAMINO, PAMINA
O return, golden hours!
Farewell, farewell!

(they part)

Papageno

Papageno

PAPAGENO
(eilt ihnen nach)
Tamino! Tamino!
Willst du mich denn gänzlich verlassen?
Wenn ich nur wenigstens wüsste,
Wo ich bin!

PAPAGENO
(hurrying after them)
Tamino! Tamino!
Would you forsake me for good?
If I only had any idea
where I was!

*(Er kommt an die Tür, wo Tamino
abgeführt worden ist)*

*(He comes to the door through
which Tamino was led away)*

EINE STIMME
Zurück!

A VOICE
Stand back!

*(Dann ein Donnerschlag: das Feuer
schlagt zur Tur heraus)*

*(A clap of thunder: flames burst
from the door)*

PAPAGENO
Barmherzige Götter! Wenn ich nur
wüsste, wo ich hereinkam!

PAPAGENO
Merciful gods! If I only knew which
way I came in!

*(Er kommt an die Türe, wo er
hereinkam)*

*(He comes to the door by which he
entered)*

DIE STIMME
Zurück!

THE VOICE
Stand back!

(Donner und Feuer wie oben)

(Thunder and flames as before)

PAPAGENO
Nun kann ich weder vorwärts noch
zurück!

PAPAGENO
Now I can't go either forwards or
backwards!

(Er weint)

(He weeps)

ZWEIUNDZWANZIGSTER AUFTRITT	SCENE 22

Papageno. Sprecher, der ihm entgegen-
tritt.

The Speaker approaches
Papageno

SPRECHER
Mensch! Du hättest verdient, auf
immer in finsteren Klüften der Erde zu
wandern. Die gütigen Götter entlassen
dich der Strafe. Dafür aber wirst du das
himmlische Vergnügen der Eingeweihten
nie fühlen.

SPEAKER
Wretched man, you deserve to
wander for ever in the dark bowels
of the earth. But the merciful gods
have remitted your punishment; yet
you shall never feel the divine joy
of the initiate.

PAPAGENO
Je nun, es gibt ja noch mehr Leute
meinesgleichen. – Mir wäre jetzt ein
gutes Glas Wein das himmlischste
Vergnügen.

PAPAGENO
Oh well, there are lots of men like
me. – The most divine joy for me at
the moment would be a good glass
of wine.

(Ein grosser Becher mit rotem Wein
kommt aus der Erde)

(A large goblet of red wine rises out
of the ground)

Juchhe! Da ist er schon! *(Trinkt)*
Herrlich!

Hurray! There it is! *(drinks)*
Splendid!

SPRECHER
Sonst hast du keinen Wunsch in dieser
Welt?

SPEAKER
Have you no other wish in this
world?

PAPAGENO
Mir wird ganz wunderlich ums Herz!
Ich möchte . . . ich wünschte . . .
Ja, was möcht' ich denn?

PAPAGENO
I've a very strange feeling in my
heart! I wish . . . I'd like . . .
now what is it?

(Sprecher ab)

(exit Speaker)

20. ARIE

20. ARIA

PAPAGENO
(Schlägt dazu sein Glockenspiel)
Ein Mädchen oder Weibchen
Wünscht Papageno sich.
O, so ein sanftes Täubchen
Wär Seligkeit für mich!
Dann schmeckte mir Trinken und Essen,
Dann könnt' ich mit Fürsten mich messen,
Des Lebens als Weiser mich freun,
Und wie im Elysium sein.

PAPAGENO
(accompanying himself on his bells)
A little maid or wife –
that's what Papageno wants.
A sweetheart would be
utter bliss for me!
Food and drink would taste better
and I wouldn't change place with a
prince; I'd enjoy life as much as any
scholar and feel I was in Heaven.

Ein Mädchen oder Weibchen
Wünscht Papageno sich.
O, so ein sanftes Täubchen
Wär Seligkeit für mich!
Ach, kann ich denn keiner von allen
Den reizenden Mädchen gefallen?
Helf' eine mir nur aus der Not,
Sonst gräm ich mich wahrlich zu Tod.

Ein Mädchen oder Weibchen
Wünscht Papageno sich.
O, so ein sanftes Täubchen
Wär Seligkeit für mich!
Wird keine mir Liebe gewähren,
So muss mich die Flamme verzehren!
Doch küsst mich ein weiblicher Mund,
So bin ich schon wieder gesund!

DREIUNDZWANZIGSTER AUFTRITT

*Papageno, Die Alte tanzend, auf ihren
Stock sich stützend*

WEIB
Da bin ich schon, mein Engel!

PAPAGENO
Du hast dich meiner erbarmt?

WEIB
Ja, mein Engel!

PAPAGENO
Das ist ein Glück!

WEIB
Und wenn du mir versprichst, mir ewig
treu zu bleiben, dann sollst du sehen, wie
zärtlich dein Weibchen dich lieben wird.

PAPAGENO
Nur nicht so hastig, lieber Engel! So ein
Bündnis braucht doch seine
überlegung.

WEIB
Papageno, ich rate dir, zaudre nicht!
Deine Hand, oder du bist auf immer
hier eingekerkert.

A little maid or wife —
that's what Papageno wants.
A sweetheart would be
utter bliss for me!
Ah, can't I please a single one
of all these pretty maids?
One must help me in my need
or I'll surely grieve to death.

A little maid or wife —
that's what Papageno wants,
A sweetheart would be
utter bliss for me!
If no one will love me
the flames of Hell will consume me!
But a kiss from a woman's lips
would cure me right away!

SCENE 23

*Enter the old woman dancing,
leaning on her stick*

WOMAN
Here I am, my love!

PAPAGENO
So you've taken pity on me?

WOMAN
Yes, love!

PAPAGENO
Isn't that a bit of luck?

WOMAN
And if you promise always to be
true to me, you shall see how
tenderly your little wife will love
you.

PAPAGENO
Not quite so fast, my dear! An
engagement like this needs thinking
over.

WOMAN
Papageno, I advise you not to delay!
Give me your hand, or you'll be
shut up here for ever.

PAPAGENO
Eingekerkert?

WEIB
Wasser und Brot wird deine tägliche
Kost sein. Ohne Freundin musst du leben
und der Welt auf immer entsagen.

PAPAGENO
Wasser trinken? Der Welt entsagen? —
Nein, da will ich doch lieber die Alte
nehmen, als gar keine. — Nun, da hast
du meine Hand darauf, das ich dir immer
getreu bleibe, *(für sich)* so lang ich keine
Schönere sehe.

WEIB
Das schwörst du?

PAPAGENO
Ja, das schwör ich!

Weib verwandelt sich in ein junges Weib,
welches ebenso gekleidet ist, wie
Papageno

PAPAGENO
Pa — Pa — Papagena!

(Er will sie umarmen)

VIERUNDZWANZIGSTER AUFTRITT

Sprecher. Die Vorigen

SPRECHER
Fort mit dir, junges Weib! Er ist deiner
noch nicht würdig! Zurück, sag
ich!

PAPAGENO
Eh' ich mich zurückziehe, soll die Erde
mich verschlingen. *(Er sinkt hinab)* Oh, ihr
Götter!

VERWANDLUNG

Ein Garten

PAPAGENO
Shut up?

WOMAN
Bread and water will be your daily
fare. You'll have to live without a
sweetheart and renounce the world
for ever.

PAPAGENO
Drink water? Renounce the world? —
No, I'd rather take the old woman
than no one. — So, there's my hand
on it; I'll always be faithful to you
(aside) until I see someone who's
prettier.

WOMAN
Do you swear it?

PAPAGENO
Yes, I swear it!

Woman is transformed into a young
woman dressed exactly like
Papageno

PAPAGENO
Pa — Pa — Papagena!

(He goes to embrace her)

SCENE 24

Enter Speaker

SPEAKER
Away with you, young woman! He
is not yet worthy of you! Back, I
say!

PAPAGENO
May the earth swallow me before I
retreat! *(He sinks into the ground)*
O, ye gods!

TRANSFORMATION

A garden

Die drei Knaben

The three boys

21. FINALE

21. FINALE

DIE DREI KNABEN
Bald prangt, den Morgen zu verkünden,
Die Sonn auf goldner Bahn!
Bald soll der Aberglaube schwinden,
Bald siegt der weise Mann.
O holde Ruhe, steig hernieder,
Kehr in der Menschen Herzen wieder;
Dann ist die Erd ein Himmelreich,
Und Sterbliche sind Göttern
gleich.

THE THREE BOYS
Soon, to herald the morn,
the sun will shine in golden
splendour! Soon superstition will
vanish and wisdom be victorious.
O sweet peace, descend on us,
return again to men's hearts;
then the kingdom of Heaven will be
on earth and mortals resemble the
gods!

ERSTER KNABE
Doch seht, Verzweiflung quält
Paminen.

1st BOY
But see, Pamina is tormented by
despair.

ZWEITER und DRITTER KNABEN
Wo ist die denn?

2nd and 3rd BOYS
Where is she?

ERSTER KNABE
Sie ist von Sinnen.

1st BOY
Out of her mind.

DIE DREI KNABEN
Sie quält verschmähter Liebe Leiden.
Lasst uns der Armen Trost bereiten!
Fürwahr, ihr Schicksal geht uns nah!
O wäre nur ihr Jüngling da! –
Sie kommt, lasst uns beiseite gehn,
Damit wir, was sie mache, sehn.
(Sie gehen beiseite)

THE THREE BOYS
The pangs of slighted love torment
her. Let us comfort the poor girl!
Indeed, her fate is our concern!
If only her fair youth were here! –
She's coming: Let us stand aside and
watch what she does.
(They withdraw)

SECHSUNDZWANZIGSTER AUFTRITT   SCENE 26

Pamina mit einem Dolch in der Hand, die Vorigen

Enter Pamina, with a dagger in her hand

PAMINA
(zum Dolch)
Du also bist mein Bräutigam?
Durch dich vollend' ich meinen Gram!

PAMINA
(to the dagger)
So you shall be my bridegroom?
Through you my grief shall be ended!

DIE DREI KNABEN
(beiseite)
Welch dunkle Worte sprach sie da?
Die Arme ist dem Wahnsinn nah.

THE THREE BOYS
(aside)
What dreadful words does she utter?
The poor girl's near to madness.

PAMINA
Geduld, mein Trauter, ich bin dein,
Bald werden wir vermählet sein.

DIE DREI KNABEN
Wahnsinn tobt ihr im Gehirne;
Selbstmord steht auf ihrer Stirne. —
Holdes Mädchen, sieh uns an!

PAMINA
Sterben will ich, weil der Mann,
Den ich nimmermehr kann hassen,
Seine Traute kann verlassen. *(Auf den
Dolch zeigend))*Dies gab meine Mutter mir.

DIE DREI KNABEN
Selbstmord strafet Gott an dir.

PAMINA
Lieber durch dies Eisen sterben,
Als durch Liebesgram verderben.
Mutter, durch dich leide ich,
Und dein Fluch verfolget mich.

DIE DREI KNABEN
Mädchen, willst du mit uns gehn?

PAMINA
Ha, des Jammers Mass ist voll!
Falscher Jüngling, lebe wohl!
Sieh, Pamina stirbt durch dich:
Dieses Eisen töte mich.

DIE DREI KNABEN
(halten ihr den Arm)
Ha, Unglückliche! Halt ein!
Sollte dies dein Jüngling sehen,
Würde er von Gram vergehen;
Denn er liebet dich allein.

PAMINA
Was? Er fühlte Gegenliebe?
Und verbarg mir seine Triebe,
Wandte sein Gesicht von mir?
Warum sprach er nicht mit mir?

PAMINA
Patience, beloved, I am thine:
soon shall we be united.

THE THREE BOYS
Madness clouds her mind;
suicide sits on her brow. —
Fair maiden, look at us!

PAMINA
I must die, since the man
whom I could never hate
can forsake his true love.
(indicating the dagger) This my
mother gave me.

THE THREE BOYS
God would punish you for suicide.

PAMINA
Rather die by this blade
than wither from love's anguish.
Mother, through you do I suffer,
and your curse pursues me.

THE THREE BOYS
Maiden, will you go with us?

PAMINA
Ah, my cup of sorrow is full!
False youth, farewell!
See, Pamina dies for you:
this blade shall despatch me.

THE THREE BOYS
(holding her by the arm)
Stop, unhappy maid!
If the youth you love should see this,
he would die of grief,
for he loves you alone.

PAMINA
What? He loves me in return
but hid his feelings from me
and turned his face away?
Why would he not speak to me?

DIE DREI KNABEN
Diese müssen wir verschweigen,
Doch wir wollen dir ihn zeigen!
Und du wirst mit Staunen sehn,
Dass er dir sein Herz geweiht,
Und den Tod für dich nicht scheut,
Komm, wir wollen zu ihm gehen.

THE THREE BOYS
This we must not divulge,
but we will show him to you;
and you will be surprised to see
that his heart is dedicated to you
and for you he would brave death.
Come, we'll go to him.

PAMINA
Führt mich hin, ich möcht ihn sehn!

PAMINA
Take me too; I must see him!

DIE DREI KNABEN
Komm, wir wollen zu ihm gehen.

THE THREE BOYS
Come, we'll go to him.

ALLE
Zwei Herzen, die vor Liebe brennen,
Kann Menschenohnmacht niemals trennen.
Verloren ist der Feinde Müh,
Die Götter selbst beschützen sie.

ALL
No human power can part
two hearts on fire with love.
Hostile threats are all in vain;
the gods themselves protect them.

VERWANDLUNG

TRANSFORMATION

*Zwei grosse Berge; in dem einen ist ein
Wasserfall, der andere speit Feuer aus.*

*Two great mountains, a waterfall on
one, the other spewing fire.*

SIEBENUNDZWANZIGSTER AUFTRITT

SCENE 27

*Zwei schwarzgeharnischte Männer,
Tamino leicht angezogen, ohne sandalen*

*Two men in black armour, Tamino
lightly clad without sandals*

DIE GEHARNISCHTEN
Der, welcher wandert diese Strasse voll
Beschwerden,
Wird rein durch Feuer, Wasser, Luft und
Erden;
Wenn er des Todes Schrecken überwinden
kann,
Schwingt er sich aus der Erde himmelan.
Erleuchtet wird er dann imstande sein,
Sich den Mysterien der Isis ganz zu weihn.

THE MEN IN ARMOUR
He who treads this path of trials
must traverse fire, water, air and
earth;

if he can overcome the fear of death
he shall soar from earth to heaven.
Then can he be enlightened
and fully devote himself to the
mysteries of Isis.

TAMINO
Mich schreckt kein Tod, als Mann zu
handeln,
Den Weg der Tugend fortzuwandeln.
Schliesst mir die Schreckenspforten auf,
Ich wage froh den kühnen Lauf.

TAMINO
Death will not deter me from acting
like a man
and following the path of virtue.
Though the gates of terror open for me
I'll gladly dare the fearful course.

(will gehen)

(He makes to enter)

PAMINA
(von innen)
Tamino, halt! Ich muss dich sehn.

TAMINO
Was hör ich? Paminens Stimme?

DIE GEHARNISCHTEN
Ja, ja, das ist Paminens Stimme.

TAMINO, DIE GEHARNISCHTEN
Wohl mir (dir), nun kenn sie mit mir (dir)
gehn, Nun trennet uns (euch) kein
Schicksal mehr,
Wenn auch der Tod beschieden wär!

TAMINO
Ist mir erlaubt, mit ihr zu sprechen?

DIE GEHARNISCHTEN
Dir ist erlaubt, mit ihr zu sprechen!

TAMINO, DIE GEHARNISCHTEN
Welch Glück, wenn wir uns (euch)
wiedersehn,
Froh Hand in Hand in Tempel gehn.
Ein Weib, das Nacht und Tod nicht scheut,
Ist würdig und wird eingeweiht.
*(Pamina wird vom zweiten Priester
hereingefuhrt; Tamino und Pamina
umarmen sich)*

PAMINA
Tamino mein! O welch ein Glück!

TAMINO
Pamina mein! O welch ein Glück!
Hier sind die Schreckenspforten,
Die Not und Tod mir dräun.

PAMINA
Ich werde aller Orten an deiner Seite sein,
Ich selber führe dich, die Liebe leitet mich.
Sie mag den Weg mit Rosen streun,
Weil Rosen stets bei Dornen sein.
Spiel du die Zauberflöte an,
Sie schütze uns auf unsrer Bahn.
Es schnitt in einer Zauberstunde
Mein Vater sie aus tiefstem Grunde
Der tausend jahr'gen Eiche aus.
Bei Blitz und Donner, Sturm und Braus.

PAMINA
(from within)
Tamino, wait! I must see you.

TAMINO
What do I hear? Pamina's voice?

THE MEN IN ARMOUR
Yes, that is Pamina's voice.

TAMINO, THE MEN IN ARMOUR
Ah joy! Now she can go with me
(you); fate no longer separates us
(you) even if death be our (your)
lot.

TAMINO
Am I allowed to speak to her?

THE MEN IN ARMOUR
You are allowed to speak to her.

TAMINO, THE MEN IN ARMOUR
What joy to meet again and in
happiness go hand in hand to the
temple.
A woman who does not fear night or
death is worthy to be considered.
*(Pamina is led in by the 2nd Priest;
Tamino and Pamina
embrace)*

PAMINA
My Tamino! O what joy!

TAMINO
My Pamina! O what joy!
Here are the gates of terror,
which threaten pain and death.

PAMINA
No matter where, I'll be at your
side; I myself will lead you, and
love will be my guide. It may strew
the path with roses, for roses go
with thorns. Play your magic flute
to protect us on our way. My father
carved it in a magic hour from the
heart of an ancient oak a thousand
years old, amid thunder and
lightning, storm and tempest. Now

89

Nun komm und spiel die Flöte an,
Sie leite uns auf grauser Bahn.

ALLE
Wir wandeln (Ihr wandelt) durch des
Tones Macht,
Froh durch des Todes düstre Nacht.

*(Tamino bläst seine Flöte. Sie
durchwandern die Feuerhöhle und
umarmen sie sich)*

PAMINA, TAMINO
Wir wandelten durch Feuergluten,
Bekämpften mutig die Gefahr.
Dein Ton sei Schutz in Wasserfluten,
So wie er es im Feuer war.

*(Sie wenden sich zur Wasserhöhle. Eine
Türe öffnet sich: man sieht einen Eingang
in einen Tempel, welcher hell erleuchtet
ist.)*

PAMINA, TAMINO
Ihr Götter! Welch ein Augenblick!
Gewähret ist uns Isis Glück.

CHOR DER PRIESTER
(von innen)
Triumph! Triumph! Du edles Paar!
Besieget hast du die Gefahr,
Der Isis Weihe ist nun dein.
Kommt, tretet in den Tempel ein!

VERWANDLUNG

Der vorige Garten

ACHTUNDZWANZIGSTER AUFTRITT

Papageno allein

PAPAGENO
(ruft mit seinem Pfeifchen)
Papagena, Papagena, Papagena!
Weibchen, Täubchen, meine Schöne!
Vergebens! Ach, sie ist verloren!
Ich bin zum Unglück schon geboren.

come, play on your flute; it shall
guide us on our perilous path.

ALL
With music as shield we (you) can
lightly step through the dark night
of death.

*(Tamino plays his flute. They pass
through the mountain of
fire and embrace each other)*

PAMINA, TAMINO
We have passed through the fiery
furnace and confidently faced
danger. May the flute's sound
protect us from the waters as it did
from the fire.

*(They pass through the water: the
gates of the temple are thrown open
and a brilliant light radiates the
scene)*

PAMINA, TAMINO
Ye gods, what glory!
Isis has granted us his favour.

CHORUS OF PRIESTS
(from within)
Triumph! Triumph, noble pair!
You have surmounted danger
and the mysteries of Isis are open
to you. Come, enter the temple!

TRANSFORMATION

The garden, as before

SCENE 28

Papageno alone

PAPAGENO
(calling on his panpipes)
Papagena, Papagena, Papagena!
Little wife, my dove, my sweet!
In vain! Alas, I've lost her!
I was born to misfortune.

Ich plauderte, und das war schlecht,
Und drum geschieht es mir schon recht.
Seit ich gekostet diesen Wein . . .
Seit ich das schöne Weibchen sah,
So brennt's im Herzenskämmerlein,
So zwickt es hier, so zwickt es da.
Papagena, Herzensweibchen!
Papagena, liebes Täubchen!
's ist umsonst, es ist vergebens!
Müde bin ich meines Lebens!
Sterben macht der Lieb ein End,
Wenn's im Herzen noch so brennt.
(nimmt einen Strick)
Diesen Baum da will ich zieren,
Mir an ihm den Hals zuschnüren,
Weil das Leben mir missfällt;
Gute Nacht, du falsche Welt.
Mir kein schönes Kind zubandelst:
So ist's aus, so sterbe ich,
Schöne Mädchen, denkt an mich.
Will sich eine um mich Armen,
Eh' ich hänge, noch erbarmen,
Wohl, so lass ich's diesmal sein!
Rufet nur: ja oder nein! –
Keine hört mich, alles stille!
Also ist es euer Wille?
Papageno, frisch hinauf! Ende deinen
Lebenslauf. – Nun, ich warte noch, es sei,
Bis man zählet eins, zwei, drei.
(pfeift)
Eins! Zwei! Drei!
Non wohlan, es bleibt dabei,
Weil mich nichts zurücke hält!
Gute Nacht, du falsche Welt.

(Er will sich hängen)

DIE DREI KNABEN
(eilen herbei)
Halt ein, O Papageno, und sei klug;
Man lebt nur einmal, dies sei dir genug.

PAPAGENO
Ihr habt gut reden, habt gut scherzen.
Doch brennt es euch wie mich im Herzen,
Ihr würdet auch nach Mädchen gehn.

DIE DREI KNABEN
So lasse deine Glöckchen klingen,
Dies wird dein Weibchen zu dir bringen.

I chattered, which was wrong,
and so it served me right.
Ever since I tasted that wine . . .
Ever since I saw my lovely little
wife, my heart has been on fire
and pierced through and through.
Papagena, wife of my heart!
Papagena, my sweet dove!
Useless! All in vain!
I'm tired of life!
Death will put an end to love
though it still burns in my heart.
(takes a rope)
I'll decorate this tree here
by hanging myself by the neck from
it; good night, perfidious world!
Since you treat me so badly
and grant me no sweetheart,
then all is over, I will die:
fair maids, think of me!
Before I hang myself, if but one
maid will take pity on me, well, I'll
let it go this time! Just say the
word, yes or no! – No one's
listening: not a sound! So that's
your will then? Papageno, get on
with it and end your life! – I'll
just wait and see until I've counted
one, two, three.
(he pipes)
One! Two! Three!
Well then, there's no help,
since nothing holds me back.
Perfidious world, good night!

(He is about to hang himself)

THE THREE BOYS
(hurrying in)
Stop, Papageno, and be sensible;
you've only one life; make the most
of it.

PAPAGENO
You can give good advice, and joke
about it but if your hearts were on fire
you'd also run after girls.

THE THREE BOYS
Then chime your bells;
they'll bring your wife to you.

PAPAGENO
Ich Narr vergass der Zauberdinge!
Erklinge, Glockenspiel, erklinge!
Ich muss mein liebes Mädchen sehn.
Klinget, Glöckchen, klinget,
Schafft mein Mädchen her!
Klinget, Glöckchen, klinget,
Bringt mein Weibchen her!

DIE DREI KNABEN
Nun, Papageno, sieh dich um!
(Sie holen Papagena und gehen ab)

PAPAGENO
Pa – Pa – Pa – Papagena!

PAPAGENA
Pa – Pa – Pa – Papageno!

PAPAGENO
Bist du mir nun ganz gegeben?

PAPAGENA
Nun bin ich dir ganz gegeben.

PAPAGENO
Nun, so sei mein liebes Weibchen!

PAPAGENA
Nun, so sei mein Herzenstäubchen!

BEIDE
Welch Freude wird das sein,
Wenn die Götter uns bedenken,
Unsrer Liebe Kinder schenken,
So liebe kleine Kinderlein!

PAPAGENO
Erst einen kleinen Papageno!

PAPAGENA
Dann eine kleine Papagena!

PAPAGENO
Dann wieder einen Papageno!

PAPAGENA
Dann wieder eine Papagena!

PAPAGENO
What a fool I was to forget my
magic charm! Ring, bells, ring!
I must see my pretty maid.
Ring, bells, ring!
Bring my sweetheart here!
Ring, bells, ring!
Bring my little wife here!

THE THREE BOYS
Now, Papageno, turn round and look!
*(They have brought in Papagena:
they themselves exeunt)*

PAPAGENO
Pa – Pa – Pa – Papagena!

PAPAGENA
Pa – Pa – Pa – Papageno!

PAPAGENO
Are you all mine now?

PAPAGENA
I'm all yours now.

PAPAGENO
Now be my dear little wife!

PAPAGENA
Now be my heart's delight!

BOTH
How delightful it will be
if the gods bless us
and crown our love with children,
such dear little children!

PAPAGENO
First a little Papageno!

PAPAGENA
Then a little Papagena!

PAPAGENO
Then another Papageno!

PAPAGENA
Then another Papagena!

BEIDE
Papagena! Papageno!
Es ist das höchste der Gefühle,
Wenn viele, viele
Pa – Pa – Pa – Papagenos
Pa – Pa – Pa – Papagena
Der Eltern Gegen werden sein.

(Beide ab)

VERWANDLUNG

Unterirdisches Gewölbe

NEUNUNDZWANZIGSTER AUFTRITT

*Monostatos. Die Königin mit ihren Damen;
sie tragen schwarze Fackeln in der Hand.*

ALLE
Nur, stille, stille, stille, stille!
Bald dringen wir im Tempel ein.

MONOSTATOS
Doch Fürstin, halte Wort! Erfülle . . .
Dein Kind muss meine Gattin sein.

KÖNIGIN
Ich halte Wort; es ist mein Wille.
Mein Kind soll deine Gattin sein.

DIE DREI DAMEN
Ihr Kind soll deine Gattin sein.

MONOSTATOS
Doch still! Ich höre schrecklich rauschen,
Wie Donnerton und Wasserfall.

KÖNIGIN, DIE DREI DAMEN
Ja, fürchterlich ist dieses Rauschen
Wie fernen Donners Widerhall.

MONOSTATOS
Nun sind sie in des Tempels
Hallen.

BOTH
Papagena! Papageno!
It will be the greatest bliss
if many, many
Pa – Pa – Pa – Papagenos
and Pa – Pa – Pa – Papagenas
shall be their parents' blessing.

(Exeunt)

TRANSFORMATION

An underground vault

SCENE 29

*Monostatos. The Queen with her
ladies carrying black torches.*

ALL
Now absolute quiet!
We'll soon gain entry to the temple.

MONOSTATOS
But Queen, keep your promise!
Your daughter must be mine.

QUEEN
I'll keep my promise: it is my will
that my daughter shall be yours.

THE THREE LADIES
Her daughter shall be yours.

MONOSTATOS
But hark! I hear a dreadful noise
like thunder or a waterfall.

QUEEN, THE THREE LADIES
Yes, fearful is that noise
like the echo of distant thunder.

MONOSTATOS
Now they are within the temple's
halls.

ALLE
Dort wollen wir sie überfallen,
Die Frömmler tilgen von der Erd'
Mit Feuersglut und Mâcht'gem
Schwert.

ALL
There we will surprise them,
and clear the earth of these
hypocrites by the night of fire and
sword.

DIE DREI DAMEN, MONOSTATOS
Dir, grosse Königin der Nacht,
Sei unsrer Rache Opfer gebracht.

THE THREE LADIES, MONOSTATOS
May our vengeance be a sacrifice
to you, great Queen of Night!

(Donner, Blitz, Sturm)

(Thunder, lightning, storm)

ALLE
Zerschmettert, zernichtet ist unsere
Macht,
Wir alle gestürzet in ewige Nacht.

ALL
Our power is shattered and destroyed
and we all are cast into endless night.

(Sie versinken)
*(Sogleich verwandelt sich das ganze
Theater in eine Sonne. Sarastro steht
erhoht; Tamino, Pamina, beide in
priesterlicher Kleidung. Neben ihnen die
ägyptischen Priester auf beiden Seiten.
Die drei Knaben halten
Blumen.)*

(They sink below)
*(Suddenly the whole stage is
transformed into a blaze of sun-
light. Sarastro stands exalted:
Tamino and Pamina are in priestly
robes. Near them, Egyptian priests
on either side. The three boys are
carrying flowers)*

DREISSIGSTER AUFTRITT

SCENE 30

Sonnentempel
*Sarastro, Tamino und Pamina, die
Priester, die drei Knaben*

The temple of the sun
*Sarastro, Tamino and Pamina,
priests, the three boys*

SARASTRO
Die Strahlen der Sonne vertreiben die
Nacht,
Zernichten der Heuchler erschlichene Macht.

SARASTRO
The sun's rays expel night and
destroy the insidious power of
hypocrisy.

CHOR DER PRIESTER
Heil sei euch Geweihten! Ihr dranget
durch Nacht!
Dank sei dir, Isis; dank dir, Osiris, gebracht!
Es siegte die Stärke und krönet zum Lohn
Die Schönheit und Weisheit mit ewiger
Kron'!

CHORUS OF PRIESTS
Hail, you enlightened souls who
penetrated the dark!
Thanks be, Isis, to you and to Osiris!
Strength has triumphed and rewarded
beauty and wisdom with an eternal
crown!

DIE ENTFÜHRUNG
AUS DEM SERAIL
(The Seraglio)

Introduction

'But Candide . . . was concerned only with his journey
to find his dear Cunégonde at Constantinople . . . He was
scarcely on board before he fell on his friend's neck
. . . "Well," Candide said to him, "what of Cunégonde?
Is she still prodigiously beautiful? Does she still love me?"'

Voltaire (1759)

The Genre

Exploration, commerce and empire gave eighteenth-century Europe
the raw material for a cult of the exotic. The influx of *objets trouvés*,
some of them human, satisfied the century's proto-scientific passion
for curios and classification, and moved the imagination of artists:
painters, including Stubbs and G.B. Tiepolo; architects, including
J. Effner (who built the chinoiserie pavilion at Nymphenburg) and
John Nash; writers such as Pope, Montesquieu and Defoe; and librettists and composers of opera, including Frederick the Great and
Mozart.

The effect made at home by travellers' tales was the opposite of
the effect intended abroad by most of the travellers. Missionaries set
out to Christianise pagans, militarists and merchants to subdue and
exploit savages. But from the information they sent back to Europe
the message read by Enlightened thought was that pagans and
savages might be more moral and more civilised than Christendom.

The taste for the exotic was the aesthetic and fictional face of a
searching intellectual comparison. It became known that other con-
tinents had religions and social systems with claims to absoluteness

just as strong as the divine revelation and the divine right of kings on which European institutions claimed to rest. Between several claims to supra-rational authority there is no rational arbitrating. So the rational course was to seek out the creative, deistical principle inherent in all religions, and to design constitutional systems of government which, instead of depending on the special revelation that your feudal lord was your absolute master, could be justified by reasoning – a process which anyone can follow, without supernatural help, with the result that government could rest on the reasoned consent of the governed.

The form of the fictitious traveller's tale, in which the traveller questions the natives about the institutions of their society and the answers cast a satirical and sceptical light on institutions at home, had been sketched by Sir Thomas More and is still in use by science fiction. In the eighteenth century Swift expanded the traveller's tale into *Gulliver's Travels* and Voltaire developed the form into his pamphlets in the shape of fictions (including his interplanetary science fiction, *Micromégas*). Mozart, at least when he was young, grieving and writing to his worried and conservative father, disliked Voltaire[1] but, six years after Voltaire's death, joined the Freemasons* – who adulated Voltaire, practised the Enlightenment's morality (including toleration) and were, for that reason, condemned (twice, during the eighteenth century) by papal bull. Catholicism declined to return Masonry's compliment of toleration because Masonry, as a 'universal' system of morality, seemed to imply that the church was not necessary to morals and because Masonry insisted (from 1723 onwards) on extending the tolerance it offered its Christian members equally to Jews and Deists.

The Style

Mozart was 25 and not yet a Mason when he was given the chance to compose an opera in German for the court theatre at Vienna – and picked a story in the Turkish sub-department of the exotic vein, concerning the rescue, quite à la *Candide*, of a sweetheart held captive in Turkey, and turning on a pagan who proves to be nobler and more tolerant than a Christian.

The text was in German thanks to a recent fashion among German rulers for replacing opera-in-Italian, which had long and excellently served their courts, by German-speaking opera – literally German-

---
* *see above*

100

speaking, because the linking dialogue was spoken, whereas the connective tissue of opera-in-Italian was sung recitative.

Recitative had come into opera for quite other reasons but it remained, I surmise, to perform a specialised function. The texts that Da Ponte wrote for Mozart and many of Metastasio's texts (which supplied Mozart among dozens of other composers) were, though in Italian and by Italians, designed for German patrons and audiences. No doubt the recitative was meant to do what it still incidentally does, namely slow down the dialogue so that it could be followed by an audience that knew Italian but wasn't born to it.

However, pride in one's Italian (which might be helped out, as it was for *Idomeneo*[2], by the publication of the Italian text together with a German translation) was for courtiers and aspirant courtiers. After its début at court, an opera composed to an Italian text was often performed elsewhere in Germany (sometimes by a commercial company) in German translation[3]. In such a performance the recitative might be replaced by spoken dialogue[4]. When opera for German courts took to German, it became free to do the same. Dialogue in the audience's native language might move as fast as speech.

The courts' shift to German and speech didn't in reality bring opera closer to German popular entertainment. The courts intended to drum up patriotism and to encourage German singers (recitative is an international skill, because a foreign accent can't be detected in it, whereas spoken dialogue needs native speakers) but they had no thought of going proletarian. Italian, German or translated, opera remained grand opera: a form distinct from popular entertainment because it demands opera singers (not just singers) and a full orchestra. Even *Die Zauberflöte*, a commercial enterprise, pop in manner, with spoken dialogue and a German text, set Mozart's sister-in-law, Josepha, who sang the Queen of the Night, the stiffest test an opera singer can take and is, as it called itself on its published libretto[5], a grand opera – 'eine grosse Oper'.

The impetus to German texts was strongest in Mannheim. Mozart, who was there in 1777, reported that an opera to a text by C.M. Wieland (the writer who was later a distant influence on *Die Zauberflöte*) owed part of its success to being 'the first German Singspiel'[6]. Mozart qualifies 'Singspiel' by 'German' because 'Singspiel' in itself didn't, as it's sometimes thought it did, imply that the text was German. 'Singspiel' was merely the German-rooted word, an alternative to 'Oper', for an opera of any kind: when the playbill was in German, even operas composed to and sung in Italian, like *Figaro* and *Così*[7], were billed as Italian Singspiele.

By 1781 the Germanising fashion had been taken up in Vienna. (Four years later it was already, to Mozart's regret[8], faltering — for want, precisely, of opera singers; the German-born singers could sing equally well with the Italian opera, but it was, presumably, harder for the German opera to call on foreign skill.) Mozart's commission of 1781 for *Die Entführung* was, according to his early biographer[9], part of Joseph II's plan, 'so worthy of a German emperor', to alienate taste from opera-in-Italian, support German singers and encourage patriotism.

Mozart's own genius was for music-dramatising the cadences of language itself. He beautifully bends to the idiom of whichever particular language he is setting. His aptitude for words, which made him a great dramatist (and a punster) also, in combination with his travelled upbringing, made him polyglot. He wrote (and signed) his letters, and inscribed friends' albums, in French, Italian, English or Latin, besides his native German, and gave evidence of his delight in his own and human language's versatility in the two-fold statement[10] he wrote in his German-Italian dictionary: an assertion that the book belonged to him made once in German in gothic script and once in Italian in roman, with his names in his two signatures rendered in the appropriate languages.

The Text

Mozart was perhaps moved towards a Turkish subject (which he exuberantly exploited — 'Osmin's rage is rendered comical', he wrote[11], 'by the use of the Turkish music') by a feeling that there was Turkish-spiced music still unexpressed in him. Two years before, he had left unfinished, because production plans went wrong, the opera now called *Zaide*, which is likewise Turkish in setting though in musical mood very different from *Die Entführung*. On 18 April 1781 Mozart told his father, about the earlier project, 'there is nothing to be done' and went on, in the same epistolary breath, to adumbrate the new: 'Stephanie junior is going to give me a new libretto, a good one, as he says'.

By June Mozart had received the imperial commission: the director of the court theatre assigned to a well-known actor the job of finding

Mozart a libretto[12]. The quest led back to 'Stephanie junior' – Gottlieb Stephanie, manager of the opera, a playwright whom Mozart suspected of plagiarism and all Vienna of double-dealing but who possessed the one virtue that mattered to Mozart: 'he still understands the stage'. Stephanie had in his possession a libretto he said would be excellent if it were altered. Mozart, warned perhaps by his experiences with *Zaide* and certainly by the poverty that was already pressing on him, reminded himself not to set pen to music-paper before the project was officially approved lest he turn out to 'have had the honour of composing for nothing'[13].

On 30 July Stephanie delivered Mozart a libretto: Stephanie's adaptation of the text by C.F. Bretzner for an opera which had been performed earlier in the year at Berlin. Within two days of getting the script Mozart had composed Constanze's first aria, Belmonte's first aria, and the trio that ends Act I[14].

In reporting that to his father, Mozart designated the arias not by the characters' but by the intended singers' names – a token of his habit of tailoring his work to exploit the virtues of the available cloth[15]. Presently he was telling his father 'I have sacrificed Constanze's aria a little to the flexible throat of Mlle Cavalieri' and 'As we have given the part of Osmin to Herr Fischer, who certainly has an excellent bass voice . . ., we must take advantage of it' – which was done by giving Osmin a couple of extra arias[16].

Mozart worked so fast partly because he believed, on 1 August, that the opera would be produced in the middle of September 1781 (in the event, it had to queue for production and didn't appear until 16 July 1782) but also because he was so pleased 'at having to compose this opera' that 'I rush to my desk with the greatest eagerness and remain seated there with the greatest delight'[17]. Vienna, whose theatre Mozart praised[18] and contrasted with Salzburg's want of theatre[19], was, he declared[20], 'for my métier the best place in the world'. And in the exercise of that métier, 'The best thing of all is when a good composer, who understands the stage and is talented enough to make sound suggestions, meets an able poet, that true phoenix'[21].

Mozart's collaboration with Stephanie, documented in the constant reports Mozart sent from Vienna to his father in Salzburg, is witness to the soundness, and the extent, of the suggestions Mozart made – by virtue of the understanding of the stage and the aptitude for words which made opera indeed his métier. Against his father's academic objections Mozart defends the stageworthiness of the words Stephanie has given Osmin. 'I am well aware the verse is not of the best', Mozart says, but it 'is perfectly in keeping with the character of stupid, surly, malicious Osmin', it 'fitted in' with 'the musical ideas which already were buzzing in my head' and in *performance*, which is to Mozart the centre of the question, 'no deficiencies will be found'[22]. Of Stephanie himself Mozart made highly specific requests. 'As the original text began with a monologue, I asked Herr Stephanie to make a little arietta out of it — and then to put in a duet instead of making the two chatter'[23]. Midway in composing, Mozart had to pause, because 'the whole story is being altered — and, to tell the truth, at my own request'. For one of Osmin's extra arias, 'I have explained to Stephanie the words I require' — and in fact Mozart must have written the words, or at least fixed their rhythm, himself, for 'I had finished composing most of the music before Stephanie knew anything whatever about it'. Stephanie was indeed 'arranging the libretto . . . as I want it — exactly'.

The Themes
Die Entführung is about love and about society.

Its two themes are linked from the outset — from the very setting out of the characters. The list slices through society and reveals the humanity common to upper and lower layers. Mozart gives the work its social tone along with its formal symmetry: by balancing (as he did again in *Die Zauberflöte* and, with more elaboration and inter-reaction, in *Figaro*) a pair of upper-class lovers with a proletarian pair.

Die Entführung touches on sexual possessiveness, the common disease of common humanity, in the Act II quartet which opens with Constanze's cry of joy, 'Ach Belmonte', but is darkly invaded by Belmonte's doubts of her. Before harmony returns to the quartet, the lovers' alliances break down and the four persons are realigned in the alliances of the sex war. The quartet enacts in brief the re-shufflings which constitute the formal pattern of *Così*.

The great question of *Così* is inner and psychological: how is one to tell whether one's feelings are infatuation or true love? That question is posed also in *Die Zauberflöte*, where Tamino at first falls in love with a mere portrait: he and Pamina together learn, in the Masonic education-by-ordeal, to solidify sexual attraction into the love that triumphs over the fear of death. *Die Entführung* raises the question less psychologically, from the outside only (how is *Belmonte* to tell whether *Constanze* truly loves him?), but returns the same triumphant answer. First Constanze is tested alone. She sings her sorrow ('Traurigkeit') with almost the free and romantic expressiveness of Pamina's 'Ach, ich fühl's' and flings her defiance at death and torture in the incandescent bravura of 'Martern aller Arten'. Then, after the failure of the rescue, she and Belmonte together pass through the fear of death, as Pamina and Tamino pass through the ordeals; and together they emerge, in the Allegro ('Ich will alles gerne leiden . . .') of their marvellously psychological duet, to affirm that, in the idea of dying together, the idea 'together' triumphs over the idea 'dying'.

Having borrowed the Enlightenment's favourite background, the exotic, *Die Entführung* enlists its favourite profession. It is by posing as, of course, an architect that Belmonte penetrates the palace — which is a stroke, simultaneously, of social versimilitude: architecture is perhaps the only useful profession (and he must pretend to be useful if he is to tempt the Pasha) which it could not bruise Belmonte's Spanish pride to assume. Building-mania was so universal that proficiency in architecture was quite consonant with landed-gentlemanliness. To the eighteenth century's beneficent and inspired mania Europe still owes (if only it can be persuaded not to pull them down in sheer philistinism) its most beautiful buildings and city-scapes. Architecture, especially in its entire sense of landscape-and-city planning, invited the Enlightenment's most imaginative investment, because it was the most patently social of the arts and at the same time the most demonstrably and mathematically rational. Not by accident was it the medieval craft-guild of the masons which re-emerged in the early eighteenth century into a second life as the incarnation of Enlightened morality. Masonic allegory makes the deistical principle the 'architect' of the universe. And Belmonte's impersonation of an architect suggests the metaphor whereby he, in his Act III aria, entrusts himself to the principle of love: 'I *build* on your power, o love'.

The Enlightened point that the most oppressed and neglected classes in human society, namely servants and women, are in reality as human as anyone else is made by Mozart by musical and dramatic means, in the artistic intensity with which he treats his female and proletarian personages. *Die Entführung's* rebuke to force and feudalism is uttered by women, one of them a serving-woman. Blonde tells Osmin to woo by being winning instead of by being conquering ('Durch Zärtlichkeit und Schmeicheln'). Constanze delivers the same message to the Pasha in the fully philosophical tones of the Enlightenment. 'Tomorrow you must love me', he says. '"Must"! Absurd desire!' she reasonably points out.

The impossibility of compelling love, whether sexual love or the love of the people for a ruler, and, in consequence, the perverse irrationality of supposing one has a right to command or forbid it, are the centre of the opera. Not that it is a propagandist work. Joseph II was welcome to construe the Pasha's change of heart (if an emperor too tone-deaf to compute that Mozart had given the music exactly the right number of notes* can be held capable of construing anything) as shewing that absolute power need not preclude magnanimity. The opera is content to demonstrate where the limits of power are reasonably set. It argues tacitly: for a constitutionalism defined by reason on the strength of the facts, including love, of the human nature shared by all classes.

Something approaching constitutional government was, through most of the eighteenth century, possessed only by the English (who got it by cutting off their king's divine and absolute head a century and a half before the French brought themselves to treat their king likewise). England was the source of the Enlightenment, and of Masonry in its Enlightened eighteenth-century form — facts which inspired anglophilia in Voltaire and in Mozart (who remarked, some three months after the first night of *Die Entführung*, 'I am an out-and-out Englishman'[24]). Enlightened anglophilia created Blonde, embodiment of English constitutionalism, a maidservant who tells off Osmin with the words 'I am an Englishwoman, born to freedom' (which provokes him to grumble, along the bass line to their ensuing duet, that English men must be henpecked).

Constanze and Belmonte are tested as to the truth of their passion, and it proves true. The Pasha, however, is tested as to the *reasonableness* of acting on his — both his passion for Constanze and his passion for revenge against Belmonte's Christian father, who has ill-used him. He ends by abandoning both his claims. He frees Belmonte because to execute vengeance can only damage the revenger's nature ('I hold your father in too much detestation to be able to tread in his footsteps') and frees Constanze because neither force nor kindness on

* *see above*

106

his part *can* alter the fact that she is not in love with him.

The conversion of Selim into a constitutionalist is accomplished offstage – and unsung. As it is put in the cast-list Mozart sent home[25] when he was beginning to compose, 'Bassa Selim – Herr Jautz: He has nothing to sing'. Perhaps Mozart was tailoring his work to skills available and not available. (Four years later, the German opera in Vienna was reduced to keeping going 'with actors and actresses, who only sing when they must'[26].) Whether out of a deficiency in the company or from his spontaneous imagination, Mozart contrived a positive item of drama and at the same time avoided the cliché of a remote act of generosity patly solving problems from on high. Because Selim's is a speaking part and therefore, in an opera, a minimal part, the sufferings by which he arrives at his generous resolution are not told to the audience but have to be supplied by the audience's sympathy. Mozart endows Selim with an impressive nobility that pomp alone could not give him – by making him the still centre at the hub of the beautifully coloured merry-go-round spun by the singing voices.

The Crisis

Mozart composed *Die Entführung* during the greatest turbulence of his life. The opera's themes are exactly those of his personal crisis: love, and a conflict with socio-political (plus, in Mozart's case, ecclesiastical) authority. Those problems brought Mozart into a further conflict – with the supreme and unique emotional authority of his life, his father, Leopold Mozart.

The beautiful symmetry of *Die Entführung* probably acts out the intensity of Mozart's wish that his own crisis be solved with justice and precision. In real life it wasn't. Mozart found some sort of intellectual resolution in Masonry, and Leopold patched up a truce by following him there*. But Mozart's relation to Leopold continued to be ambivalently pursued after Leopold's death – to which Mozart's immediate reaction was to invoke the punishment of heaven on himself through the fate of Don Giovanni, seducer, scoffer and murderer of an authoritarian father-figure. In *Die Zauberflöte* Mozart was still reconciling himself to paternal authority (Sarastro) by submitting himself to the Masonic symbolic death-by-ordeal. Sarastro, however, is an Enlightened authority. Though seeming at first not to, he endorses the love of Tamino and Pamina. Leopold Mozart

* *see above*

107

never did the equivalent. There was no resolution to Mozart's relation to him until Mozart died too.

At the beginning of 1781 both Mozarts held musical appointments at the court of Salzburg, whose ruler was Prince-Archbishop Hieronymus Colloredo. Mozart had gone, on leave of absence, to Munich, where in January 1781 he launched his opera-in-Italian *Idomeneo*. From Munich he was, in March, ordered directly to Vienna, to join the retinue (which didn't include Leopold) accompanying the Archbishop of Salzburg on a visit[27] to Vienna.

Mozart had long been unhappy in Salzburg. Its theatres were insufficient either to entertain him or to promote his talent for opera, and its musical audiences were as unappreciative as 'tables and chairs'[28]. At Vienna Mozart lived as part of the Archbishop's household, but not a cherished part: he lunched with the cooks at a table presided over by the valets[29]. (Mozart's complaint perhaps fell tactlessly on Leopold Mozart, who had begun his career as valet plus musician to a count.) The Archbishop paid Mozart a salary he couldn't live on but often refused him permission to earn by other means[30] or even to give his services for charity[31]. Determined to stop 'burying my youth and my talents in Salzburg'[32], Mozart planned to resign from the Salzburg service and stay on in Vienna, where, he believed, he could make a better living by giving concerts and taking pupils[33] and stood a strong chance of an operatic commission[34].

This plan Mozart detailed to his father by post, imploring Leopold to consent. Leopold had no more liking for their common employer than Mozart had. But Leopold was prepared to put up with the terms of service. His son's refusal to do the same Leopold interpreted as a coldness towards himself. All his adult life, whenever he was separated from his father, Mozart had faithfully remitted accounts of his doings, for Leopold's criticism, plus as much money as he could, by overworking, scrape together for Leopold's support. ('You must be content with very little this time . . . Had I foreseen this event, I should have taken the pupils who wanted to come to me'[35].) Leopold now accused him of never having shewn him any affection. Mozart made the agonised reply that in the tone of Leopold's letter he failed to recognise his father — and put forward, in vain, the conciliatory suggestion that Leopold, too, should settle in Vienna[36].

At the beginning of May the Archbishop's household began to pack up to return to Salzburg. Mozart, turned out of the house without warning, was taken in as a lodger by the musical family Weber, whom he had known in Mannheim. The Archbishop ordered him back to Salzburg; Mozart, now that the Archbishop was no longer providing his keep, needed first to collect money due to him in Vienna; so he put off his departure by two days. The result, on 9 May, was a stand-up row. The Archbishop, addressing him in the idiom used by noblemen to servants, called him a bad servant and shouted at him to clear out[37].

Mozart presented his resignation – which had to go through Count Arco, the Archbishop's Malvolio, who held it up for a month and then expelled Mozart from the Archbishop's antechamber with a kick in the arse. Mozart reiterated his resignation in a memorandum to the Archbishop – who replied by dismissing him[38].

Leopold Mozart ('You really are too timid', Mozart wrote[39] to him) was terrified: that the affair would damage him, Leopold (though Mozart assured him there had been no threats and that the Archbishop had in any case no power to harm him)[40]; that Mozart would get, among the Viennese upper class, a name for insubordination[41]; and that Mozart was indeed rebelling against the subordinate situation of artists – which was true. Mozart was fevered and trembling[42] with indignation at the personal and social injustice inflicted on him. 'I hate the Archbishop to madness', he wrote[43]. Against Count Arco he longed for revenge but promised himself merely to get exactly even, and not go beyond that into punishing his enemy, in words like the Pasha's (which he hadn't yet read): 'I should be placing myself on a level with him, and really I am too proud to measure myself with such a stupid booby'. No doubt he alarmed Leopold by the revolutionist tone of his comment: 'though I am no count, yet I have probably more honour in me than many a count'[44].

Leopold feared that Mozart was turning not merely revolutionist but profligate. Mozart sent assurances that he was keeping up Catholic observance and not associating with prostitutes[45]. In deference to gossip and to his father[46], he moved out of his lodgings with the Webers. For Madame Weber, now widowed, had four[47] daughters.

With the second daughter, Aloysia, Mozart had been (as he now freely told his father[48]) foolishly in love; but she had become a famous opera singer, turned Mozart down and married Josef Lange, actor (and painter of an unfinished portrait of Mozart). In July 1781

Mozart affirmed[49] to his father 'I am not in love with' the 'middle' Weber girl, who bore the name of the heroine of the opera he was about to compose, Constanze. But a fortnight later, when he began to compose, Mozart misreported the opera's title to Leopold: his pen wrote 'seduction' instead of 'abduction'[50]. Had Leopold been as acute a psychologist as Mozart and Da Ponte when they made Susanna let slip the truth by singing 'Yes' when she had intended to tell the lie 'No'[51], he might have foreseen the information Mozart sent him in December, that he meant to marry Constanze.

Having wooed Constanze (who in the course of his courtship threw him over thrice[52]) Mozart wooed Leopold by letter to the idea of her. He presented her as thrifty, shabby and 'far from beautiful' and his own motives as the need for a relief from concupiscence (which Leopold so dreaded in him) and someone to look after his clothes[53]. In the fact that the guardian of the fatherless Constanze had obliged Mozart to sign a contract to marry or indemnify her, he could find no winning face to present to Leopold except that Constanze herself, trusting him, had torn up the document[54].

In July 1782 Mozart sent his father word of the good reception of *Die Entführung*[55], evidence, it must have seemed, that he had been right to move to Vienna. Now he was imploring Leopold's consent[56] to another of his decisions. For the second time Leopold refused to set him free. Constanze's constancy was tested, and Mozart's love for her proved, in the ordeal by cold fire of Leopold's unwillingness. In August, with the help of Mozart's friend and patron the Baroness von Waldstädten, the couple tumbled hastily into marriage, having waited for but not received Leopold's consent (which arrived the next day)[57]. It was an elopement: not for the bride but for the bridegroom. Leopold Mozart must have felt as sad, forsaken and broken of his power as the Pasha would have done had the abduction succeeded instead of being overtaken by his generosity.

BRIGID BROPHY

[1] Mozart wrote his outburst against Voltaire at 22, on the day his mother died, in a letter which concealed the news of her death from his father (from Paris, 3 July 1778). Four days earlier Leopold Mozart had written Mozart *his* anti-Voltaire outburst. But during Mozart's child-prodigy tour, Leopold intended (in 1766) to take Mozart to visit Voltaire – who was, however, ill (O.E. Deutsch, p.59, p.66). Conceivably, the French revolutionary writer Mozart read later in his life (O.E. Deutsch, p.539) was Voltaire.
    [2] O.E. Deutsch, p.190.   [3] Cf., e.g. O.E. Deutsch, p.224, p.343.
[4] So I conclude from a report of 1791 (O.E. Deutsch, p.392) which says that in a Berlin *Don Giovanni* 'There is little speaking'.
[5] – whose title-page is reproduced in *Mozart und seine Welt . . .*, p.253.   [6] 'dass erste teütsche singspiel' (3 December 1777).   [7] The first-production playbills are reproduced on p.198 and p.231 of *Mozart und seine Welt . . .*   [8] Mozart's letter (to a Mannheim dramatist) of 21 May 1785.
    [9] F.X. Niemetschek, 1808.   [10] – in 1785; reproduced on p.190 of *Mozart und seine Welt . . .*   [11] 26 September 1781.
    [12] Letter of 9 June 1781.   [13] Letter of 16 June.   [14] Letters of 1 August and 6 October 1781, and E. Anderson's footnotes.
    [15] Mozart (28 February 1778): 'I like an aria to fit a singer as perfectly as a well made suit of clothes'. Leopold Mozart (24 November 1770): 'Wolfgang . . . has only composed one aria for the primo uomo, because . . . Wolfgang . . . prefers to wait for his arrival so as to fit the costume to his figure'.   [16] Letter of 26 September 1781.
    [17] 1 August 1781.   [18] Mozart to his sister, 4 July 1781.   [19] 26 May 1781.   [20] 4 April 1781.
    [21] 13 October 1781.   [22] 13 October 1781.   [23] This and the quotations in the remainder of the paragraph are from Mozart's letter of 26 September 1781.   [24] ' . . . dass ich ein ErzEngelländer bin' (19 October 1782).   [25] Letter of before 26 September 1781.
    [26] 21 May 1785.   [27] The Archbishop's Viennese visit began in January (E. Anderson, p.713). Leopold Mozart had been with Mozart in Munich, where he stayed on a few days after Mozart's departure, before returning to Salzburg.   [28] 26 May 1781.   [29] 17 March.   [30] 17 March and 4 April.   [31] 24 March.   [32] 11 April.

[33] 8 April. [34] 28 April and 26 May.
[35] 2 June. [36] 19 May. [37] 9 May. [38] 9 June. [39] 4 July. [40] 2 June.
[41] 9 May. [42] 12 May.
[43] 9 May. [44] 20 June. [45] 13 June. [46] 25 July and 5 September.
[47] — at the least: Mozart's letter of 17 January 1778 mentions 'five girls and one son'. [48] 16 May 1781. [49] 25 July. [50] *Verführung* instead of *Entführung* (1 August 1781).

[51] — in 'Crudel, perchè finora' in *Le Nozze di Figaro*. [52] Mozart's letter to Constanze Weber of 29 April 1782. [53] 15 December 1781. [54] 22 December 1781. [55] 20 July. [56] 27 July 1782. [57] Letter of 7 August 1782.

DIE ENTFÜHRUNG AUS DEM SERAIL
(The Seraglio)

Libretto by
Gottlieb Stephanie the younger
after
C. F. Bretzner

DRAMATIS PERSONAE

PASHA SELIM
CONSTANZE, *loved by Belmonte*
BLONDE, *her English maid*
BELMONTE, *a young Spanish nobleman*
PEDRILLO, *his servant, now the Pasha's gardener*
OSMIN, *overseer of the Pasha's estate*
CAPTAIN OF THE WATCH
A DUMB MAN

CHORUS of Janissaries, watchmen, slaves, etc.

*The opera is set on the Pasha's seaside estate in Turkey,
and the action is contained within a single day.*

Synopsis

ACT I

Outside the Pasha's palace by the sea. Belmonte, in search of his lost sweet-heart, asks Osmin if this is Pedrillo's place of work. The very name arouses Osmin's ire, and he chases Belmonte away. Pedrillo himself enters to see if the Pasha is back, and receives a sample of Osmin's bile: his anger is aroused mainly by Pedrillo's ogling of the harem women. Once Osmin has left, Belmonte re-enters and is united with Pedrillo. The latter has written to Belmonte telling him how he, Constanze and Blonde were captured by corsairs and sold to the Pasha — this is the reason for Belmonte's arrival. The Pasha has fallen in love with Constanze, but she remains faithful to Belmonte. A ship has been procured for their escape but Pedrillo advises extreme caution.

The Pasha and Constanze return from a sea trip, and the Pasha ardently renews his suit. Constanze reminds him of her love for another, and retires. Pedrillo introduces Belmonte to the Pasha as an architect, and he is ordered to report for duty the next day. Belmonte and Pedrillo manage to evade the watchful Osmin and slip into the palace.

ACT II

The garden of the Pasha's palace. Osmin, who has been given Blonde as a slave by the Pasha and imagines he can order her about, is given a sharp lecture on how different things are in England. He retires in discomfort. The Pasha tells Constanze that his patience is running out and that she must learn to love him. He even threatens torture and death, and when she proudly pours scorn on the very notion he wonders whether her very confidence betrays hopes of escape. Pedrillo brings Blonde the good news of Belmonte's arrival and tells her that she and her mistress must be ready to leave at midnight. Pedrillo now gets Osmin drunk — not too arduous a task — and the coast is clear for a reunion. This is marred only by Belmonte's tactless enquiry as to whether Constanze has remained true to him, a question echoed by Pedrillo to Blonde. Pedrillo gets a box on the ear for his pains, and Constanze's pained reaction is enough to convince Belmonte. All is forgotten and forgiven.

ACT III

In front of the palace. With the help of a sailor from Belmonte's ship, Pedrillo secures the ladders. He sings a serenade beneath Constanze's window, and she soon climbs down and hurries away with Belmonte. But after Pedrillo has climbed into Blonde's window, a dumb guard rouses Osmin and all four are caught red-handed. As they are led away to the Pasha, Osmin's triumph is alarmingly bloodthirsty.

A room in the Palace. The Pasha reproaches Constanze for betraying his trust. She nobly offers to die in Belmonte's place, but when the Pasha discovers that Belmonte is the son of his oldest enemy, the man responsible for his exile from Algeria and the loss of his own true love, his anger knows no bounds. He leaves with Osmin to prepare orders for their torture and death.

Belmonte and Constanze determine to face death with calm joy, but when the Pasha returns, he announces that he despises Belmonte's father far too much to follow his example and that he will repay injustice with mercy. All four are to go free, much to Osmin's fury. All join in praise of the Pasha's noble forbearance and remark, with reference to Osmin's storming exit, that nothing is so hateful as revenge.

Erster Aufzug

Act one

ERSTER AUFZUG

Platz vor dem Palast des Bassa Selim am Ufer des Meeres. Den Hintergrund nimmt eine Terrasse ein. Rechts ist ein Flügel des Palastes sichtbar, zu dessen Eingang einige Stufen führen. Auf der linken Seite ein Feigenbaum mit einer daran gelehnten Leiter.
Belmonte allein.

1. ARIE

BELMONTE
Hier soll ich dich denn sehen,
Konstanze, dich mein Glück!
O Himmel, hör mein Flehen,
gib mir die Ruh' zurück!
Ich duldete der Leiden,
O Liebe, allzuviel.
Schenk mir dafür nun Freuden
und bringe mich ans Ziel.
(gesprochen)
Aber wie soll ich in den Palast kommen?
Wie sie sehen, wie sprechen?

(Er bemerkt den sich nahenden Osmin und zieht sich beobachtend zurück. Osmin, mit einem Körbchen in der Hand, besteigt die Leiter am Feigen baum und legt die abgenommenen Früchte in das Körbchen.)

2. LIED UND DUETT

ACT ONE

In front of the Pasha Selim's palace on the seashore. There is a terrace at the back; a wing of the palace is visible on the right, with a flight of steps leading to it; on the left, a fig-tree with a ladder leaning against it.
Belmonte alone.

1. ARIA

BELMONTE
Here then shall I see you,
Constanze, my joy!
O heaven, hear my pleas
and restore my peace!
O love, I have suffered
all too many sorrows.
Now grant me joys in their stead
and bring me to my goal.
(spoken)
But how am I to get into the palace?
How am I to see her and speak to her?

(He notices Osmin approaching and withdraws to watch, Osmin, carrying a basket, climbs up the ladder on the fig-tree and picks fruit into the basket.)

2. SONG AND DUET

OSMIN
Wer ein Liebchen hat gefunden,
die es treu und redlich meint,
lohn' es ihr durch tausend Küsse,
mach' ihr all das Leben süsse,
sei ihr Tröster, sei ihr Freund.
Trallalera, trallalera!

BELMONTE
(gesprochen)
Vielleicht, dass ich durch diesen Alten
etwas erfahre. He, Freund! Ist das
nicht das Landhaus des Bassa
Selim?

OSMIN
(singt wie zuvor während der Arbeit)
Doch sie treu sich zu erhalten,
schliess' er's Liebchen sorglich ein;
denn die losen Dinger haschen
jeden Schmetterling und naschen
gar zu gern von fremden Wein.
Trallalera, trallalera!

BELMONTE
(gesprochen)
He, Alter, he! Hört Ihr nicht? Ist hier
des Bassa Selim Palast?

OSMIN
*(sieht ihn an, dreht sich gleichgültig
herum und singt wie zuvor)*
Sonderlich beim Mondenscheine,
Freunde, nehmt sie wohl in acht!
Oft lauscht da ein junges Herrchen,
kirrt und lockt das kleine Närrchen,
und dann, Treue, gute Nacht!
Trallalera, trallalera!

BELMONTE
Verwünscht seist du samt deinem Liede!
Ich bin dein Singen nun schon müde;
so hör doch nur ein einzig Wort!

OSMIN
Was Henker lasst Ihr Euch gelüsten,
Euch zu ereifern, Euch zu brüsten?
Was wollt Ihr? Was wollt Ihr?
Hurtig! Ich muss fort.

OSMIN
He who has found a sweetheart
true and faithful to him
should reward her with a thousand
kisses and sweeten her whole life,
be her comfort and her friend.
Trallalera, trallalera!

BELMONTE
(spoken)
Perhaps I can find out something
from this old man. Hey, friend!
Isn't this the Pasha Selim's country
house?

OSMIN
(continuing to sing as he works)
But to keep her faithful, let him
carefully lock his sweetheart in;
for the flighty creatures snatch
at every butterfly, and all too
gladly sip at others' wine.
Trallalera, trallalera!

BELMONTE
(spoken)
Hey, old fellow, hey! Don't you hear
me? Is this the Pasha Selim's palace?

OSMIN
*(having looked at him, turns back
unconcernedly and continues singing)*
Above all when the moon is shining,
friends, keep a watchful eye on her!
Some fine young gentleman is often
lurking, luring and tempting the
silly girl, and then good night to
fidelity! Trallalera, trallalera!

BELMONTE
A pox on you and your song!
I'm tired of your singing;
just listen to a word!

OSMIN
Why do you get yourself so worked
up, so excited, so puffed up?
What d'you want? What is it then?
Hurry! I must go.

BELMONTE
Ist das des Bassa Selim Haus?

BELMONTE
Is this the Pasha Selim's house?

OSMIN
He?

OSMIN
Eh?

BELMONTE
Ist das des Bassa Selim Haus?

BELMONTE
Is this the Pasha Selim's house?

OSMIN
Das ist des Bassa Selim Haus.

OSMIN
This is the Pasha Selim's house.

(will fort)

(makes to leave)

BELMONTE
So wartet doch!

BELMONTE
Just a moment though!

OSMIN
Ich kann nicht weilen.

OSMIN
I can't dilly-dally here.

BELMONTE
Ein Wort!

BELMONTE
One word!

OSMIN
Geschwind, denn ich muss eilen.

OSMIN
Be quick, I'm in a hurry.

BELMONTE
Seid Ihr in seinen Diensten, Freund?

BELMONTE
Are you in his service, friend?

OSMIN
He?

OSMIN
Eh?

BELMONTE
Seid Ihr in seinen Diensten, Freund?

BELMONTE
Are you in his service, friend?

OSMIN
Ich bin in seinen Diensten, Freund.

OSMIN
I am in his service, friend.

BELMONTE
Wie kann ich den Pedrill wohl sprechen,
der hier in seinen Diensten steht?

BELMONTE
How can I speak to Pedrillo,
who works for him here?

OSMIN
Den Schurken, der den Hals soll brechen?
Seht selber zu, wenn's anders geht.

OSMIN
That scoundrel, whose neck I'd
like to wring. Find him yourself
if you want him.

BELMONTE
(Was für ein alter, grober Bengel!)

BELMONTE
(What a churlish old boor!)

OSMIN
(Das ist just so ein Galgenschwengel!)

BELMONTE
Ihr irrt, Ihr irrt,
es ist ein braver Mann.

OSMIN
So brav, so brav,
dass man ihn spiessen kann.

BELMONTE
Ihr müsst ihn wahrlich nicht recht kennen.

OSMIN
Recht gut! Ich liess' ihn heut verbrennen.

BELMONTE
Es ist fürwahr ein guter Tropf!

OSMIN
Auf einen Pfahl gehört sein Kopf!

(will fort)

BELMONTE
So bleibet doch!

OSMIN
Was wollt Ihr noch?

BELMONTE
Ich möchte gerne - -

OSMIN
(spöttisch)
So hübsch von ferne ums Haus
rumschleichen und Mädchen stehlen?
Fort, Euresgleichen braucht man
hier nicht.

BELMONTE
Ihr seid besessen, sprecht voller Galle
mir so vermessen ins Angesicht!

OSMIN
Nur nicht in Eifer!

BELMONTE
Schont Euren Geifer.

OSMIN
(This is a gallows-bird just like him!)

BELMONTE
You're wrong, you're wrong,
he's an honest man.

OSMIN
So honest, so honest,
that I'd impale him on a spit.

BELMONTE
You can't know him properly.

OSMIN
Can't I! I'd have him roasted today.

BELMONTE
He's really a good chap!

OSMIN
His head should be stuck on a pike!

(makes to leave)

BELMONTE
Just a moment!

OSMIN
What is it now?

BELMONTE
I'd like to - -

OSMIN
(scornfully)
. . . to come skulking round the
house and steal the girls? Off
with you, we don't want your
sort here.

BELMONTE
You're demented, to affront me
to my face with such rancour!

OSMIN
Don't get so heated!

BELMONTE
Spare me your venom.

OSMIN
Ich kenn Euch schon.

BELMONTE
Lasst Euer Drohn.

OSMIN
Schert Euch zum Teufel! Ihr kriegt,
ich schwöre, sonst ohne Gnade
die Bastonade! Noch habt Ihr Zeit!

(drängt Belmonte hinaus)

BELMONTE
Es ist kein Zweifel, Ihr seid von Sinnen!
Welch ein Betragen auf meine Fragen!
Seid doch gescheit!

(gesprochen)

OSMIN
Könnt ich mir doch noch so einen
Schurken auf die Nase setzen, wie den
Pedrillo; so einen Gaudieb, der Tag und
Nacht nichts tut, als nach meinen Weibern
herumzuschleichen und zu schnobern,
ob's nichts für seinen Schnabel setzt.
Aber ich laure ihm sicher auf den Dienst,
und wohl bekomm dir die Prügelsuppe,
wenn ich dich einmal beim Kanthaken
kriege! Hätt' er sich nur beim Bassa nicht
so eingeschmeichelt, er sollte den Strick
längst um den Hals haben.

PEDRILLO
(kommt von rechts vorn)
Nun, wie steht's, Osmin? Ist der Bassa
noch nicht zurück?

OSMIN
Sieh danach, wenn du's
wissen willst.

PEDRILLO
Schon wieder Sturm im Kalender? Hast
du das Gericht Feigen für mich gepflückt?

OSMIN
Gift für dich, verwünschter
Schmarotzer!

OSMIN
I know your kind.

BELMONTE
Don't threaten me!

OSMIN
Go to the devil! Or I swear
you'll be awarded the bastinado
without mercy! There's still time!

(pushes Belmonte away)

BELMONTE
There's no doubt you're out of
your mind! What a reply to my
question! Do use some sense!

(spoken)

OSMIN
As if I needed yet another knave
under my feet like Pedrillo - -
a rogue who does nothing, day
or night, but prowl around my
harem sniffing out if there's
anything for him. But I'm up
to his games, and Heaven help
him if ever I catch him! If he
hadn't wormed his way into
the Pasha's favour he'd have
had the rope round his neck
long since.

PEDRILLO
(entering from the right)
How goes it, Osmin? Isn't the
Pasha back yet?

OSMIN
Look for yourself, if you want
to know.

PEDRILLO
Outlook stormy again? Did you
pick those figs for me?

OSMIN
For you poison, you pestilential
parasite!

PEDRILLO
Was in aller Welt ich dir nur getan
haben muss, dass su beständig mit
mir zankst? Lass uns doch einmal
Friede machen.

OSMIN
Friede mit dir? Mit so einem
schleichenden, spitzbübischen Passauf,
der nur spioniert, wie er mir ein versetzen
kann? Erdrosseln möcht ich dich!

PEDRILLO
Aber sag nur, warum, warum?

OSMIN
Warum? Weil ich dich nicht leiden kann.

3.   ARIE

OSMIN
Solche hergelaufne Laffen,
die nur nach den Weibern gaffen,
mag ich für den Teufel nicht;
denn ihr ganzes Tun und Lassen
ist uns auf den Dienst zu passen;
doch micht trügt kein solch Gesicht.
Eure Tücken, eure Ränke,
eure Finten, eure Schwänke
sind mir ganz bekannt.
Mich zu hintergehen
müsst ihr früh aufstehen,
ich hab auch Verstand.
Drum, beim Barte des Propheten!
ich studiere Tag und Nacht,
dich so mit Manier zu töten,
nimm dich, wie du willst, in acht.

(gesprochen)

PEDRILLO
Was bist du für ein grausamer
Kerl! Ich hab dir doch nichts
getan!

OSMIN
Du hast ein Galgengesicht,
das ist genug.

(sung)

PEDRILLO
What in the world have I ever
done to you, that you're always
quarrelling with me? Let's make
peace for once.

OSMIN
Peace with you? With a slippery
snooping sneak like you who's
only spying how to upset me?
I'd like to strangle you!

PEDRILLO
But just tell me why, why?

OSMIN
Why? Because I can't stand you.

3.   ARIA

OSMIN
These profligate puppies
who do nothing but ogle women
I simply can't abide;
for all they ever do
is watch us at our work;
but a face like that doesn't
deceive me. Your tricks, your
wiles, your schemes, your
guiles, all are known to me.
You'll have to get up early
to get the better of me;
for I know what's what.
Yes, by the beard of the Prophet,
I'll not rest, day or night,
till I find a good way to do away
with you, watch out how you may.

(spoken)

PEDRILLO
What a bloodthirsty monster you
are! And I've not done anything
to you!

OSMIN
You've the face of a gallows-bird,
that's enough.

(sung)

Erst geköpft, dann gehangen,
dann gespiesst auf heisse Stangen,
dann verbrannt, dann gebunden,
dann getaucht; zuletzt geschunden.

*(Er lässt die Leiter stehen und
geht mit dem Körbchen in den
Palast ab)*

(gesprochen)

PEDRILLO
Geh nur, verwünschter Aufpasser; es ist
noch nicht aller Tage Abend. Dir
misstrauischem, gehässigem
Menschenfeinde eine Grube zu graben,
sollte ein wahres Fest für mich sein.

(Belmonte kommt von links hinten zurück)

BELMONTE
Pedrillo, guter Pedrillo!

PEDRILLO
Ach mein bester Herr! Ist's möglich?
Sind Sie's wirklich? Schon verzweifelte
ich, ob einer meiner Briefe Sie
getroffen hätte.

BELMONTE
Sag, guter Pedrillo, lebt meine
Konstanze noch?

PEDRILLO
Lebt, und noch, hoff ich, für Sie.
Seit dem schrecklichen Tage, an welchem
das Glück uns einen so hässlichen Streich
spielte und unser Schiff von den
Seeräubern erobern liess, haben wir
mancherlei Drangsal erfahren.
Glücklicherweise traf sich's noch, dass
der Bassa Selim uns alle drei kaufte:
Ihre Konstanze nämlich, meine Blonde
und mich. Konstanze ward seine
auserwählte Geliebte.

BELMONTE
Ah! Was sagst du?

First beheaded, then hanged,
then impaled on red-hot spikes,
then burned, then bound,
then submerged, finally flayed.

*(He leaves the ladder standing
and takes the basket into the
palace)*

(spoken)

PEDRILLO
Good riddance, you damned
watchdog! We'll see who has the
last laugh. To lay a trap for you,
you suspicious, spiteful misanthrope,
would give me real pleasure.

(Belmonte returns from the left)

BELMONTE
Pedrillo, my good Pedrillo!

PEDRILLO
My dear master! Is it possible?
Is it really you? I was beginning
to despair of my letters reaching
you.

BELMONTE
Tell me, good Pedrillo, is my
Constanze alive?

PEDRILLO
Alive and still, I hope, yours.
Since that dreadful day when
fate played us a dirty trick
and let our ship be captured by
pirates, we've suffered many
hardships. Fortunately it
happened that the Pasha Selim
bought all three of us, that's to
say your Constanze, my Blonde
and me. Constanze has become
his chosen favourite.

BELMONTE
Eh! What are you saying?

PEDRILLO
Nun, nur nicht so hitzig! Sie ist noch
nicht in die schlimmsten Hände gefallen.
Der Bassa hat noch so viel Delikatesse,
keine seiner Weiber zu seiner Liebe zu
swingen; und so viel ich weisse, spielt er
noch immer den unerhörten Liebhaber.
Unter uns gesagt: ich hab auch einen Stein im
Brett beim Bassa. Durch mein bischen
Geschick in der Gärtnerei hab ich seine
Gunst weggekriegt, und dadurch hab ich
so ziemlich Freiheit, die tausend andere
nicht haben würden. Da sonst jede
Mannsperson sich entfernen muss, wenn
eine seiner Weiber in den Garten kommt,
kann ich bleiben; sie reden sogar mit mir,
und er sagt nichts darüber.

BELMONTE
Ist's möglich? Du hast sie gesprochen?
O sag, sag! Liebt sie mich
noch?

PEDRILLO
Dass Sie daran zweifeln! Ich dächte,
Sie kennten die gute Konstanze
mehr als zu gut, hätten Proben ihrer
Liebe. Doch damit dürfen wir uns
gar nicht aufhalten. Hier ist bloss
die Frage, wie's anzufangen ist, hier
wegzukommen?

BELMONTE
O da hab ich für alles gesorgt! Ich hab
hier ein Schiff in einiger Entfernung
vom Hafen, das uns auf den ersten Wink
einnimmt, und . . .

PEDRILLO
Ah! sachte, sachte! Erst müssen wir die
Mädels haben, ehe wir zu Schiffe gehen,
und das geht nicht so husch-husch wie
Sie meinen!

BELMONTE
O lieber, guter Pedrillo, mach nur, dass
ich sie sehen, dass ich sie sprechen kann!
Das Herz schlägt mir vor Angst und
Freude!

PEDRILLO
Now don't get excited! She might
have fallen into worse hands. The
Pasha still has enough delicacy not
to force his love on any of his
women, and so far as I know he's
still playing the unrequited lover.
But between ourselves I'm well in
with the Pasha. Through my modest
skill in gardening I've won his
favour, and through that a fair
amount of freedom which a
thousand others don't enjoy. Even
though every male has to withdraw
when any of his women come into
the garden, I can stay: they even
chat to me, and he doesn't mind.

BELMONTE
Is it possible? You've spoken with
her? Tell me, do: does she still love
me?

PEDRILLO
How could you doubt it? I'd have
thought you knew her too well
for that and had proof enough of
her love. But we can't waste more
time on that. The real question
now is, how do we get away from
here?

BELMONTE
Oh, I've taken care of everything.
I have a ship just outside the
harbour ready to take us aboard
at a moment's notice, and . . .

PEDRILLO
Easy, easy! Before we reach the
ship we have to get the girls, and
that's not like falling off a log,
as you think!

BELMONTE
Dear good Pedrillo, just arrange
for me to see her and speak to
her! My heart is throbbing with
anxiety and joy!

124

PEDRILLO

Pfiffig müssen wir das Ding anfangen.
Bleiben Sie hier in der Nähe. Jetzt wird
der Bassa bald von einer Lustfahrt auf
dem Wasser zurückkommen. Ich will Sie
ihm als einen geschickten Baumeister
vorstellen, denn Bauen und Gärtnerei
sind seine Steckenpferde. Aber lieber,
goldner Herr, halten Sie sich in
Schranken; Konstanze ist bei ihm . . .

BELMONTE

Konstanze bei ihm? Was sagst du?
Ich soll sie sehen?

PEDRILLO

Gemach, gemach ums Himmels willen,
lieber Herr, sonst stolpern wir! Ah, ich
glaube, dort seh ich sie schon angefahren
kommen. Gehn Sie nur auf die Seite, wenn
er kommt; ich will ihm entgegen gehen.

(geht ab)

4.   ARIE

BELMONTE

Konstanze! Konstanze!
Dich wieder zu sehen, dich!
O wie ängstlich, o wie feurig
klopft mein liebevolles Herz!
Und des Wiedersehens Zähre
lohnt der Trennung bangen Schmerz.
Schon zittr' ich und wanke,
schon zag ich und schwanke;
es hebt sich die schwellende Brust!
Ist das ihr Lispeln?
Es wird mir so bange!
War das ihr Seufzen?
Es glüht mir die Wange!
Täuscht mich die Liebe?
War es ein Traum?

PEDRILLO

(kommt hurtig gelaufen: gesprochen)
Geschwind, geschwind auf die Seite und
versteckt! Der Bassa kommt.

PEDRILLO

We need to be very fly. You stay
close at hand. The Pasha's coming
back shortly from a boating trip.
I'll introduce you to him as a
talented architect, since building
and gardening are his hobbies.
But dear, good master, keep
yourself in check: Constanze is
with him . . .

BELMONTE

Constanze with him? What are you
saying? Am I to see her?

PEDRILLO

Easy, easy, dear master, for
heaven's sake, or we're done for!
Ah, I think I see them coming.
Just make yourself scarce when he
arrives: I'll go and meet him.

(exit)

4.   ARIA

BELMONTE

Constanze, Constanze!
To see you again!
O how eagerly, o how ardently
my lovesick heart is beating!
But the joy of our reunion
will erase the anxious pain of
separation. I already tremble and
waver, quake and falter:
my breast swells to bursting!
Is that her whisper?
I'm all on fire.
Was that her sigh?
My cheeks are glowing.
Does love deceive me?
Was it a dream?

PEDRILLO

(entering hurriedly: spoken)
Quick, withdraw and hide! The
Pasha's coming.

(Belmonte und Pedrillo eilen nach rechts vorn ab. Frauen des Bassa kommen aus dem Palast und nehmen auf der rechten Seite Aufstellung. Würdenträger des Hofes nahen sich von hinten und empfangen den Bassa, an der Landungstelle. Janitscharen in Waffen marschieren von links vorn auf und nehmen auf der linken Seite Aufstellung. Sklaven erscheinen von links vorn und treten hinter die Janitscharen. Bassa Selim fährt mit Konstanze in einem Schiffe von links herbei, steigt aus, und ist Konstanze beim Aussteigen behilflich.)

5. CHOR

JANITSCHAREN
Singt dem grossen Bassa Lieder,
töne, feuriger Gesang;
und vom Ufer halle wieder
unsrer Lieder Jubelklang!
Weht ihm entgegen, kühlende Winde,
ebne dich sanfter, wallende Flut!
Singt ihm entgegen, fliegende Chöre,
singt ihm der Liebe Freuden ins Herz!

(Die Frauen des Bassa, die Würdenträger, die Janitscharen und die Sklaven entfernen sich hinten)

(gesprochen)

SELIM
Immer noch traurig, geliebte Konstanze? Immer in Tränen? Sieh, dieser schöne Abend, diese reizende Gegend, meine zärtliche Liebe für dich. Sag, kann nichts von allem dich endlich beruhigen, endlich dein Herz rühren? Sieh, ich könnte befehlen, könnte grausam mit dir verfahren, dich zwingen.
(Konstanze seufzt)
Aber nein, Konstanze, dir selbst will ich dein Herz zu danken haben, dir selbst!

KONSTANZE
Grossmütiger Mann! O dass ich es könnte, dass ich's erwidern könnte ... aber ...

(Belmonte and Pedrillo hurry off to the right. The Pasha's women come out of the palace and range themselves on the right. Court dignitaries appear from the back and greet the Pasha at the landing-stage. Janissaries in armour march forward from the left and take up positions on the left. Slaves appear from the left and range themselves behind the Janissaries. The Pasha Selim with Constanze arrives from the left by boat, alights and assists Constanze to alight.)

5. CHORUS

JANISSARIES
Raise songs to our great Pasha,
lift your voices in acclaim; .
and from the shore
let the joyous sound of our songs
re-echo. Waft him before you,
cooling breezes, flow more gently,
turbulent waters! Greet him with
song, heavenly choirs, and tell him
of the joy of love in your heart!

(The Pasha's women, the Court dignitaries, the Janissaries and slaves retire)

(spoken)

SELIM
Still sad, beloved Constanze? Still in tears? See this lovely evening, this charming spot, my tender love for you. Can nothing of all this bring you peace and move your heart? You know I could command you, treat you harshly, force you.
(Constanze sighs)
But no, Constanze, I want you yourself to give me your heart.

CONSTANZE
Generous man! If only I could, if only I could return your love ... but ...

126

SELIM
Sag, Konstanze, was hält
dich zurück?

KONSTANZE
Du wirst mich hassen.

SELIM
Nein, ich schwöre dir's. Du weisst,
wie sehr ich dich liebe, wieviel
Freiheit ich dir vor allen meinen
Weibern gestatte, dich wie meine
einzige schätze.

KONSTANZE
O so verzeih!

6. ARIE

KONSTANZE
Ach ich liebte, war so glücklich,
kannte nicht der Liebe Schmerz;
schwur ihm Treue, dem Geliebten,
gab dahin mein ganzes Herz!
Doch wie schnell schwand meine Freude,
Trennung war mein banges Los;
und nun schwimmt mein Aug' in Tränen,
Kummer ruht in meinem Schoss.

(sie geht ab)

(gesprochen)

SELIM
Ihr Schmerz, ihre Tränen, ihre
Standhaftigkeit bezaubern mich immer
mehr. Wer wollte gegen ein solches Herz
Gewalt brauchen? Nein, Konstanze,
nein: auch Selim hat ein Herz, auch
Selim kennt Liebe!

*(Belmonte und Pedrillo nahen sich vor
rechts vorn)*

PEDRILLO
Herr, verzeih, dass ich es wage, dich in
deinen Betrachtungen zu stören.

SELIM
Was willst du, Pedrillo?

SELIM
Tell me, Constanze, what holds
you back?

CONSTANZE
You will hate me for it.

SELIM
No, I swear it. You know how
much I love you, how much more
freedom I allow you than all my
other wives, how I cherish you
as my only love.

CONSTANZE
Forgive me!

6. ARIA

CONSTANZE
Ah, I was in love, and so happy,
knowing nothing of the pain of
love; I swore to be true to my
beloved and gave him my whole
heart. But how quickly my joy
vanished, separation was my
unhappy lot; and now my eyes
brim o'er with tears, sorrow
dwells in my bosom.

(exit)

(spoken)

SELIM
Her grief, her tears, her
steadfastness, enchant still
more. Who could use force against
such a heart? No, Constanze, no:
Selim too has a heart, Selim too
knows love.

*(Belmonte and Pedrillo approach
from the right)*

PEDRILLO
Forgive me, my lord, for daring
to disturb your meditations.

SELIM
What is it, Pedrillo?

PEDRILLO
Dieser junge Mann, der in Italien studierte, hat von deiner Macht, von deinem Reichtum gehört und kommt her, dir als Baumeister seine Dienste anzubieten.

BELMONTE
Herr, könnte ich so glücklich sein, durch meine geringen Fähigkeiten deinen Beifall zu verdienen!

SELIM
Hm! Du gefällst mir. Ich will sehen, was du kannst.
(zu Pedrillo)
Sorge für seinen Unterhalt. Morgen werde ich dich wieder rufen lassen.

(geht ab)

PEDRILLO
Ha! Triumph, Triumph, Herr! Der erste Schritt war getan.

BELMONTE
O wenn es möglich wäre, sie zu sprechen . . .

PEDRILLO
Wir wollen sehen, was zu tun ist. Kommen Sie nur mit mir in den Garten, aber um alles in der Welt vorsichtig und fein. Denn hier ist alles Aug und Ohr.

(Sie wollen in den Palast, Osmin kommt ihnen in der Tür entgegen und hält sie zurück)

OSMIN
Wohin?

PEDRILLO
Hinein.

OSMIN
(zu Belmonte)
Was will das Gesicht?
Zurück mit dir, zurück!

PEDRILLO
This young man, who studied in Italy, has heard of your power and wealth and has come to offer his services as an architect.

BELMONTE
Sir, would that I could be so fortunate as to earn your approval with my humble talents.

SELIM
Hm! I like the look of you. I will see what you can do.
(to Pedrillo)
See to his needs. I will send for you again tomorrow.

(exit)

PEDRILLO
Ha! Victory, victory, master! That was the first step.

BELMONTE
If only it were possible to speak to her . . .

PEDRILLO
We'll see what can be done. Come with me into the garden, but for pity's sake do be careful' there are eyes and ears everywhere.

(They are about to go into the palace, but Osmin meets them at the door and bars the way)

OSMIN
Where are you going?

PEDRILLO
Inside.

OSMIN
(to Belmonte)
And what do you want?
Back you go, back!

PEDRILLO
Gemach, Meister Grobian, gemach!
Er ist in des Bassa Diensten.

OSMIN
In des Henkers Diensten mag er sein!
Er soll nicht herein!

PEDRILLO
Er soll aber herein!

OSMIN
Kommt mir nur einen Schritt
über die Schwelle . . .

BELMONTE
Unverschämter! Hast du nicht mehr
Achtung für einen Mann meines Standes?

OSMIN
Ei, ihr mogt mir vom Stande sein! Fort,
fort, oder ich will euch Beine
machen.

PEDRILLO
Alter Dummkopf! Es ist ja der Baumeister,
den der Bassa angenommen hat.

OSMIN
Meinethalben sei er Stockmeister, nur
komm er mir nicht zu nahe. Der Bassa
ist weich wie Butter, mit dem könnt ihr
machen was ihr wollt, aber ich habe eine
feine Nase. Gaunerei ist's um den ganzen
Kram, mit euch fremden Gesindel.

PEDRILLO
Ereifere dich nicht so, Alter, er hilft dir
doch nichts. Sieh, soeben werden wir
hinein spazieren.

OSMIN
Ha, das will ich sehen!
(stellt sich vor die Tür)

PEDRILLO
Mach keine Umstände.

BELMONTE
Weg, Niederträchtiger!

PEDRILLO
Easy on, you old grouch! He's in
the Pasha's service.

OSMIN
He can be in the hangman's service:
he's not coming in.

PEDRILLO
He certainly is coming in.

OSMIN
Take just one step over the
threshold . . .

BELMONTE
How dare you! Have you no respect
for a man of my position?

OSMIN
I don't give a fig for your position!
Off with you, or I'll help you on
your way.

PEDRILLO
You old fool! This is the architect
the Pasha has just engaged.

OSMIN
For all I care he can be a jailer; he'd
better not come too near me. The
Pasha's as soft as butter and you can
mould him how you like, but I've a
nose for things. The whole lot of
you foreign rabble are cheats.

PEDRILLO
Don't get so worked up, old chap,
it won't help you. Just watch us
walk in.

OSMIN
Ha! We'll see about that!
(plants himself in front of the door)

PEDRILLO
Don't make a fuss.

BELMONTE
Out of the way, sirrah!

7. TERZETTO

OSMIN
Marsch! Marsch! Marsch!
Trollt euch fort!
Sonst soll die Bastonade
euch gleich zu Diensten stehn!

BELMONTE & PEDRILLO
Ei, ei, ei!
Das wär ja Schade
mit uns so umzugehn!

OSMIN
Kommt nur nicht näher.

BELMONTE & PEDRILLO
Weg von der Türe.

OSMIN
Sonst schlag' ich drein.

BELMONTE & PEDRILLO
Wir gehn hinein!

OSMIN
Marsch fort!

BELMONTE & PEDRILLO
Platz fort!

(Sie stossen Osmin fort und gehen hinein)

7. TERZETTO

OSMIN
March, march, march!
Take yourselves off,
or you'll find the bastinado
will be at your service!

BELMONTE & PEDRILLO
Oh, oh, oh!
You'd regret it
if you treated us like that!

OSMIN
Don't come any nearer.

BELMONTE & PEDRILLO
Stand away from the door.

OSMIN
You'll feel my fist.

BELMONTE & PEDRILLO
We're going in!

OSMIN
Be off with you!

BELMONTE & PEDRILLO
Make way!

(They push Osmin aside and go in)

Zweiter Aufzug

Act two

ZWEITER AUFZUG

Garten am Palast des Bassa Selim. Rechts vorn eine Bank: etwas mehr zurückstehend ein grosser, dichtbelaubter Baum. Im Hintergrund ist ein Flügel des Palastes sichtbar.
Osmin und Blonde.

BLONDE
(gesprochen)
O des Zankens, Befehlens und Murrens wird auch kein Ende! Einmal für allemal: das steht mir nicht an! Denkst du alter Murrkopf etwa eine türkische Sklavin vor dir zu haben, die bei deinen Befehlen zittert? O da irrst du dich sehr! Mit europäischen Mädchen begegnet man ganz anders.

8.   ARIE

BLONDE
Durch Zärtlichkeit und Schmeicheln,
Gefälligkeit und Scherzen,
erobert man die Herzen
der guten Mädchen leicht.
Doch mürrisches Befehlen
und Poltern, Zanken, Plagen
macht, dass in wenig Tagen
so Lieb' als Treu' entweicht.

ACT TWO

Garden of the Pasha Selim's palace. In the foreground, right, a bench: further back is a large tree with thick foliage. In the background a wing of the palace can be seen.
Osmin and Blonde.

BLONDE
(spoken)
O there's no end to these rows, orders and grumbles! Once and for all, I'm not having it! Do you think, you old bully, that you have some Turkish slave here who trembles at your commands? You're sadly mistaken. You have to treat European girls quite differently.

8.   ARIA

BLONDE
With tenderness and coaxing,
kindness and gaiety,
it is easy to win
a gentle maiden's heart.
But boorish commands,
bluster, abuse and scolding
will very quickly banish
both love and faithfulness.

131

OSMIN
Zärtlichkeit? Schmeicheln? Hier sind
wir in der Türkei, und da geht's aus einem
andern Tone. Ich dein Herr, du meine
Sklavin; ich befehle, du musst
gehorchen!

BLONDE
Deine Sklavin? Ich deine Sklavin?

OSMIN
Du hast doch wohl nicht vergessen, dass
dich der Bassa mir zur Sklavin geschenkt
hat?

BLONDE
Mädchen sind keine Ware zum
verschenken! Ich bin eine Engländerin,
zur Freiheit geboren und trotz jedem,
der mich zu etwas zwingen will!

OSMIN
Bei meinem Bart, sie ist toll!
Hier, hier in der Türkei . . .?

BLONDE
Türkei hin, Türkei her! Lass mich nur
einmal Fuss hier gefasst haben, sie sollen
bald anders werden.

OSMIN
Freilich, wenn ich Pedrillo wär, so ein
Drahtpüppchen wie er, da wär ich
vermutlich willkommen, denn euer
Mienenspiel hab ich lange weg.

BLONDE
Erraten, guter Alter, erraten! Das kannst
du dir wohl einbilden, dass mir der
niedliche Pedrillo lieber ist, wie dein
Blasebalggesicht!

OSMIN
Gift und Dolch! Nun reisst mir die
Geduld. Den Augenblick hinein ins
Haus! Und wenn du's wagst . . .

BLONDE
Mach mich nicht lachen.

OSMIN
Tenderness? Coaxing? This is
Turkey, and here we dance to a
different tune. I'm the master,
you're my slave; I command, you
must obey!

BLONDE
Your slave? I your slave?

OSMIN
You haven't forgotten that the
Pasha gave you to me as my
slave?

BLONDE
Girls aren't goods to be given away!
I'm an Englishwoman, born to
freedom, and Britons never, never
shall be slaves!

OSMIN
By my beard, she's crazy!
Here, here in Turkey . . . ?

BLONDE
O, Turkey this and Turkey that!
Let me once get my footing here
and things will be very different.

OSMIN
Of course, if I were Pedrillo or a
puny puppet like him I'd probably
be welcome. I've had my eye on
you two for some time.

BLONDE
That's right, grandpa! You can be
quite sure that handsome Pedrillo
is dearer to me than your bellows
of a face!

OSMIN
Fire and fury! My patience is
exhausted. Into the house this
moment! And if you dare . . .

BLONDE
Don't make me laugh.

OSMIN
Ins Haus, sag ich! Mach nicht, dass ich
Gewalt brauche.

BLONDE
Gewalt were ich mit Gewalt
vertreiben. Meine Gebieterin
ist die Geliebte des Bassa,
sein Augapfel; und es kostet
mich ein Wort, so hast du
fünfzig auf die Fussohlen.

OSMIN
(für sich)
Das ist ein Satan! Ich muss nachgeben,
so wahr ich ein Muselmann bin; sonst
könnte ihre Drohung eintreffen.

9.   DUETT

OSMIN
Ich gehe, doch rate ich dir,
den Schurken Pedrillo zu meiden.

BLONDE
Fort, pack dich, befiehl nicht mit mir,
du weisst ja, ich kann es nicht leiden.

OSMIN
Versprich mir . . .

BLONDE
Was fällt dir da ein!

OSMIN
Zum Henker . . .

BLONDE
Fort, lass mich allein.

OSMIN
Beim Allah, ich werde nicht gehen,
bis du zu gehorchen mir schwörst.

BLONDE
Nicht so viel, das sollst du bald sehen,
und wenn du der Grossmogul wärst.

OSMIN
Inside, I say! Don't make me
use force!

BLONDE
I'll meet force with force.
My mistress is the Pasha's beloved, the
apple of his eye; it wants only a
word from me, and you'll get
fifty of the best on the soles of
your feet.

OSMIN
(to himself)
She's a fiend! I shall have to give
in, as true as I'm a Moslem, or she'll
carry out her threat.

9.   DUET

OSMIN
I'll go, but take my advice and stay
away from that rogue Pedrillo.

BLONDE
Be off with you, don't order me
about; you know that I won't stand
it.

OSMIN
Promise me . . .

BLONDE
The very idea!

OSMIN
Damnation!

BLONDE
Go away and leave me alone.

OSMIN
By Allah, I won't go
until you swear to obey me.

BLONDE
Not likely, you'll soon find, not
even if you were the Great Mogul.

OSMIN
(O Engländer! Seid ihr nicht Toren,
Ihr lasst euren Weibern den Willen!)

BLONDE
(Ein Mädchen zur Freiheir geboren
lässt niemals sich sklavisch befehlen,
und ist auch die Freiheit verloren,
doch bleibt sie noch Fürstin der Welt!)

OSMIN
(Wie ist man geplagt und geschoren,
wenn man so ein Früchtchen erhält!)

BLONDE
Nun troll dich!

OSMIN
So sprichst du mit mir?

BLONDE
Nicht anders.

OSMIN
Nun bleib ich erst hier!

BLONDE
Ein andermal! Jetzt musst
du gehen.

OSMIN
Wer hat solche Frechheit gesehen?

BLONDE
*(stellt sich, als wolle sie ihm die
Augen auskratzen)*
Es ist um die Augen geschehen,
wofern du noch länger verweilst.

OSMIN
Nur ruhig, ich will ja gern gehen,
bevor du gar Schläge erteilst.

*(Blonde drängt Osmin nach links hinten
hinaus. Konstanze nähert sich langsam
von rechts vorn, ohne Blonde zu
bemerken.*

10. REZITATIV UND ARIE

OSMIN
(O Englishmen! What fools you are
to let your women have their way!)

BLONDE
(A girl born to freedom will never
slavishly take orders, and even
when freedom is lost she remains
monarch of all she surveys!)

OSMIN
(How plagued and harassed one is
when one gets a hussy like this!)

BLONDE
Now off you go!

OSMIN
Is this how you speak to me?

BLONDE
How else?

OSMIN
Then I'll stay here.

BLONDE
Some other time! Now get away
with you.

OSMIN
Who ever saw such insolence?

BLONDE
*(making as if to scratch his eyes
out)*
You'll get your eyes stratched out
if you stay here any longer.

OSMIN
Gently now, I'll be going
before you lay about you.

*(Blonde pushes Osmin out, back
left. Constanze approaches slowly,
front right, without noticing
Blonde.)*

10. RECITATIVE AND ARIA

KONSTANZE
Welcher Wechsel herrscht in meiner Seele
seit dem Tag, da uns das Schicksal
trennte! O Belmonte! Hin sind die
Freuden, die ich sonst an deiner Seite
kannte! Banger Sehnsucht Leiden wohnen
nun dafür in der beklemmten Brust.

Traurigkeit ward mir zum Lose,
weil ich dir entrissen bin.
Gleich der wurmzernagten Rose,
gleich dem Gras im Wintermoose
welkt mein banges Leben hin.
Selbst der Luft darf ich nicht sagen
meiner Seele bittern Schmerz,
denn, unwillig ihn zu tragen,
haucht sie alle meine Klagen
wieder in mein armes Herz.
(gesprochen)

KONSTANZE
How my soul has been affected
since the day when fate parted us!
O Belmonte! Those joys which
once I knew at your side have fled.
The pangs of aching yearning have
replaced them in my afflicted breast

Sorrow has become my lot,
for I am torn from you.
Like the cankered rose,
like grass in winter moss,
my sad life withers away.
Even to the breeze I cannot tell
my soul's bitter anguish,
for, unwilling to carry it,
it breathes all my laments
back into my poor heart.
(spoken)

BLONDE
Ach mein bestes Fräulein, noch immer
so traurig?

BLONDE
O my dear lady,
still so sad?

KONSTANZE
Kannst du fragen, die du meinen Kummer
weisst? Wieder ein Abend, und noch
keine Nachricht, noch keine Hoffnung!
Und morgen - - ach Gott, ich darf nicht
daran denken!

CONSTANZE
Can you ask, you who know my
sorrow? One more evening, and
still no news, no hope! And
tomorrow - - oh God, I dare not
think of it!

BLONDE
Ich verzage mein Lebtag nicht, es mag
auch eine Sache noch so schlimm
aussehen. Wie bald kann Ihr Belmonte
mit Lösegeld erscheinen oder uns listiger
Weise entführen? . . . Dort seh ich den
Bassa.

BLONDE
I never give up hope, however
black things may seem. Who knows,
your Belmonte might soon appear
with the ransom or find some
ingenious way of spiriting us out . . .
I see the Pasha.

KONSTANZE
Lass uns ihm aus den Augen gehn.

CONSTANZE
Let us escape his eye.

BLONDE
Zu spät: er hat Sie schon gesehen.
(Im Weggehen)
Courage, wir kommen gewiss noch in
unsre Heimat!

BLONDE
Too late: he's already seen you.
(going)
Courage, my lady, we'll get
home yet!

(Bassa Selim kommt herein)

(Enter the Pasha Selim)

SELIM

Nun, Konstanze, denkst du meinem
Begehrn nach? Der Tag ist bald verstrichen.
Morgen musst du mich lieben, oder . . .

KONSTANZE

Muss? Welch albernes Begehren! Als ob
man die Liebe anbefehlen könnte wie
eine Tracht Schläge! Ich werde stets
so denken wie jetzt: dich verehren, aber . .
lieben? Nie!

SELIM

Und du zitterst nicht vor der Gewalt,
die ich über dich habe?

KONSTANZE

Nicht im geringsten. Sterben ist alles, was
ich zu erwarten habe, und je eher dies
geschieht, je lieber wird es mir sein.

SELIM

Nein! Nicht sterben, aber Martern
von allen Arten . . .

KONSTANZE

Auch die will ich ertragen; du schreckst
mich nicht, ich erwarte alles.

11. ARIE

KONSTANZE

Marten aller Arten
mögen meiner warten,
ich verlache Qual und Pein.
Nichts soll mich erschüttern,
nun dann würd ich zittern
wenn ich untreu könnte sein.
Lass dich bewegen, verschone mich,
des Himmels Segen belohne dich!
Doch du bist entschlossen,
willig, unverdrossen,
wähl ich jede Pein und Not.
Ordne nur, gebiete,
lärme, tobe, wüte,
zuletzt befreit mich doch der Tod.

(entfernt sich)

(gesprochen)

SELIM

Well, Constanze, have you thought
it over? The day is almost over.
Tomorrow you must love me, or . . .

CONSTANZE

Must? Absurd demand! As if one
could order love like a beating!
I shall always think as I do now:
I can respect you, but . . . love
you? Never!

SELIM

And you do not tremble before
the power I wield over you?

CONSTANZE

Not in the least. Death is all I
have to expect, and the sooner it
comes the more welcome it will be.

SELIM

No! Not death, but torture of
every kind . . .

CONSTANZE

That too I will bear. You cannot
frighten me: I await the worst.

11. ARIA

CONSTANZE

Torture of every kind
may await me;
I scorn torment and pain.
Nothing shall shake my resolve;
I would tremble only
if I were untrue to him.
If you are moved to pity and
spare me, may heaven's blessing
reward you! But if you are
adamant, callous and obdurate,
I will choose pain and torment.
Then order, command,
bluster, roar and rage;
in the end death will set me free.

(exit)

(spoken)

SELIM
Ist das ein Traum? Wo hat sie auf einmal
den Mut her, sich so gegen mich zu
betragen? Also, was Drohen und Bitten
nicht vermögen, soll die List zuwege
bringen.

(geht ab)

BLONDE
(tritt ein)
Kein Bassa, keine Konstanze mehr da?
Sind sie miteinander eins worden?
Schwerlich, das gute Kind hängt zu
sehr an ihrem Belmonte!

PEDRILLO
(tritt ein)
Bst, bst! Blondchen! Ist der Weg rein?

BLONDE
Komm nur, komm! Der Bassa ist wieder
zurück. Und meinem Alten habe ich
eben den Kopf ein bischen gewaschen.
Was hast du denn?

PEDRILLO
Neuigkeiten, Neuigkeiten, die dich
entzücken werden.

BLONDE
Nun? Hurtig heraus damit!

PEDRILLO
Belmonte, Konstanzes Geliebter, ist
angekommen, und ich hab ihn unter
dem Namen eines Baumeisters hier
im Palast eingeführt.

BLONDE
Ah, was sagst du? Belmonte da? Das muss
Konstanze wissen!

(will fort)

PEDRILLO
Hör, nur, Blondchen, hör nur erst: Er
hat ein Schiff hier in der Nähe in
Bereitschaft, und wir haben beschlossen,
euch diese Nacht zu entführen.

SELIM
Is this a dream? Where does she
suddenly get the courage to oppose
me? Well, what threats and pleas
cannot bring about I will achieve
by guile.

(exit)

BLONDE
(entering)
The Pasha and Constanze both gone?
Have they come to an understanding?
Surely not: the poor girl is too
devoted to her Belmonte!

PEDRILLO
(entering)
Pst, pst! Blonde! Is the coast clear?

BLONDE
Come on, come on! The Pasha's
gone away again; and I've just sent
my old dodderer off with a flea in
his ear. What is it?

PEDRILLO
News, news that will
delight you.

BLONDE
Well? Out with it!

PEDRILLO
Constanze's beloved Belmonte has
arrived, and I've introduced him
into the palace in the guise of an
architect.

BLONDE
What are you saying? Belmonte
here? I must tell Constanze!

(makes to go)

PEDRILLO
Listen, Blonde, just a minute!
He has a ship in readiness nearby,
and we've decided to carry you
off this very night.

137

BLONDE
O allerliebst, Herzens-Pedrillo, das
verdient einen Kuss! Geschwind,
geschwind zu Konstanze!

(will fort)

PEDRILLO
Halt nur, halt, und lass erst mit dir
reden. Um Mitternacht kommt Belmonte
mit einer Leiter zu Konstanzes Fenster,
und ich zu dem deinigen, und dann
geht's heidi davon! Leb wohl, Herzchen,
leb wohl!

(geht ab)

BLONDE
Leb wohl, guter Pedrillo! Ach, was werd
ich für Freude anrichten!

12. ARIE

BLONDE
Welche Wonne, welche Lust
regt sich nun in meiner Brust!
Voller Freude will ich springen,
ihr die frohe Nachricht bringen;
und mit Lachen und mit Scherzen
ihrem schwachen, feigen Herzen
Freud und Jubel prophezeihn.

(eilt ab)

(gesprochen)

PEDRILLO
(kommt zurück)
Ah, dass es schon vorbei wäre! Dass wir
schon auf offner See wären, unsre
Mädels im Arm und dies verwünschte
Land im Rücken hätten! Doch sei's
gewagt: entweder jetzt oder niemals.
Wer zagt, verliert!

13. ARIE

BLONDE
O dear, darling Pedrillo, that
deserves a kiss! I must fly to
Constanze.

(makes to go)

PEDRILLO
Wait a moment, wait and let me
tell you. At midnight Belmonte
will come with a ladder to
Constanze's window and I to
yours, and then off we go!
Goodbye, dearest, goodbye!

(exit)

BLONDE
Goodbye, Pedrillo dear. What
glad news I have to give!

12. ARIA

BLONDE
What bliss, what rapture
now reigns in my heart!
I could jump for joy
as I bring the good news,
and with laughter and jest
prophesy delight and jubilation
to her poor despairing heart.

(hurries out)

(spoken)

PEDRILLO
(returning)
If it were only all over! If we were
already on the open sea, with our
girls in our arms and this accursed
land behind us! Well, let's risk it:
now or never! He who hesitates
is lost!

13. ARIA

PEDRILLO
Frisch zum Kampfe! Frisch zum Streite!
Nur ein feiger Tropf verzagt.
Sollt' ich zittern, sollt' ich zagen?
Nicht mein Leben mutig wagen?
Nein, ach nein, es sei gewagt!

(gesprochen)

OSMIN
(tritt ein)
Ha! Geht's hier so lustig zu?
Es muss die verteufelt wohl
gehen.

PEDRILLO
Ei, wer wird so ein Kopfhänger sein?
Wahrhaftig, da hat euer Vater Mahomet
einen verzweifelten Bock geschossen, dass
er euch den Wein verboten hat. Wenn das
verwünschte Gesetz nicht wäre, du
müsstest ein Gläschen mit mir trinken.

OSMIN
Wein mit dir? Ja, Gift . . .

PEDRILLO
Immer Gift und Dolch, und Dolch
und Gift! Lass doch den alten Groll
einmal fahren und sei vernünftig.
Sieh einmal, ein paar Flaschen
Cyperwein! Ah!
*(zeigt ihm zwei Flaschen, wovon die
eind grösser als die andere ist)*

OSMIN
(Wenn ich trauen dürfte?)

PEDRILLO
Das ist ein Wein, das ist ein Wein!
*(Er setzt sich nach türkischer Art auf
die Erde und trinkt aus der kleinen
Flasche)*

OSMIN
Kost einmal die grosse Flasche auch.

PEDRILLO
Denkst wohl gar, ich habe Gift hinein
getan? Da sieh, ob ich trinke.

PEDRILLO
Into the fray! Into battle!
Only faint-hearts are afraid.
Should I tremble, should I waver?
Should I not boldly risk my life?
No, no: let me be resolute!

(spoken)

OSMIN
(entering)
Ha! Are you having a good time
here? Things must be
going devilishly well for you.

PEDRILLO
Why be such a misery? Really,
your father Mahomet was barking
up the wrong tree when he forbade
you to drink wine. If it weren't
for that stupid law, you could
drink a little glass with me.

OSMIN
Drink with you? Ha, fire and fury!

PEDRILLO
Oh, you and your fire and fury!
Forget your old grudges just for
once and be sensible. Look, here
are a couple of bottles of Cyprus
wine
*(shows him two bottles, one
larger than the other)*

OSMIN
(If only I dared!)

PEDRILLO
What a wine, what a wine!
*(He sits on the ground, Turkish
fashion, and drinks from the
smaller bottle)*

OSMIN
Take a drink from the big bottle too.

PEDRILLO
Do you really think I've put poison
in it? Watch me drink.

(Er trinkt aus der grossen Flasche ein wenig)
Pfui, Osmin, sollst dich schämen!
Da nimm!
(gibt ihm die grosse Flasche)
Oder willst due die kleine?

OSMIN
Nein, lass nur, lass nur! Aber wenn du mich verrätst . . .
(sieht sich sorgfältig um)

PEDRILLO
Als wenn wir einander nicht weiter brauchten. Immer frisch!

14. DUETT

PEDRILLO
Vivat Bacchus! Bacchus lebe!
Bacchus war ein braver Mann!

OSMIN
Ob ich's wage? Ob ich trinke?
Ob's wohl Allah sehen kann?

PEDRILLO
Was hilft das Zaudern?
Hinunter, nicht lange gefragt!

OSMIN
Nun wär's geschehen, nun wär's hinunter!
Das heiss ich gewagt!

PEDRILLO & OSMIN
Es leben die Mädchen,
die Blonden, die Braunen,
sie leben hoch!

PEDRILLO
Das schmeckt trefflich!

OSMIN
Das schmeckt herrlich!

PEDRILLO & OSMIN
Ach, das heiss ich Göttertrank!

OSMIN
Vivat Bacchus, Bacchus lebe,
Bacchus, der den Wein erfand!

(He takes a sip from the big bottle)
Shame on you, Osmin!
Here, take it!
(giving him the big bottle)
Or do you want the small one?

OSMIN
No, never mind! But if you give me away . . .
(looks around cautiously)

PEDRILLO
As if we wouldn't need each other later on. Drink up!

14. DUET

PEDRILLO
Vivat Bacchus! Long live Bacchus!
Bacchus was a worthy man!

OSMIN
Shall I risk it? Shall I dare?
Supposing Allah sees me?

PEDRILLO
What's the good of hesitating?
Down with it, without further question!

OSMIN
Well, I've done it, now it's down!
That's what I call daring!

PEDRILLO & OSMIN
Hurrah for girls,
fair and dark ones,
long life to them!

PEDRILLO
That tastes splendid!

OSMIN
That tastes marvellous!

PEDRILLO & OSMIN
I call that a drink fit for the gods!

OSMIN
Vivat Bacchus! Long live Bacchus!
Bacchus, who invented wine!

PEDRILLO & OSMIN
Vivat Bacchus, Bacchus lebe,
Bacchus, der den Wein erfand!

(gesprochen)

PEDRILLO
Wahrhaftig, das muss ich gestehen, es
geht doch nichts über den Wein! Wein
ist mir lieber, als Geld und Mädchen.
Bin ich verdriesslich, mürrisch, launisch,
hurtig nehm ich meine Zuflucht zur
Flasche, und kaum seh ich den ersten
Boden: weg ist all mein Verdruss!
Schwatzt mir von Süssigkeiten der Liebe
und des Ehestandes, was Ihr wollt:
Wein auf der Zunge geht über alles!

OSMIN
*(fängt bereits an, die Wirkung
des Weins und des Schlaftrunks
zu spüren, und wird bis zum
Ende des Auftritts immer
schläfriger und träger)*
Das ist wahr. Wein - - Wein ist ein
schönes Getrank - - nicht - -
Bruder Pedrillo?

PEDRILLO
Richtig, Bruder Osmin, richtig!

OSMIN
Man wird gleich so - - munter
(er nickt zuweilen)
- - so vergnügt - - so aufgeräumt.
Hast du nichts mehr, Bruder?
*(Er langt nach der zweiter Flasche,
die Pedrillo ihm reicht)*

PEDRILLO
Hör du, Alter, trink mir nicht zu viel,
es kommt einem in den Kopf.

OSMIN
Trag doch keine Sorge, ich bin so - -
nüchtern wie möglich. Aber das ist wahr - -
*(er fängt an, auf der Erde hin und
her zu wanken)*
es schmeckt - - vortrefflich!

PEDRILLO & OSMIN
Vivat Bacchus! Long live Bacchus!
Bacchus, who invented wine!

(spoken)

PEDRILLO
Well, I must say, there's nothing
to beat wine! Wine's dearer to me
than money or women. If I'm
depressed, cross or out of humour,
I take refuge in the bottle, gulp it
down, and away go all my troubles!
Say what you like about the
sweetness of love and of
matrimony, the taste of wine
beats the lot!

OSMIN
*(already beginning to feel the
effects of the wine and the
sleeping draught, and becoming
increasingly sleepy and sluggish
as the scene progresses)*
That's true. Wine - - wine's a
beautiful drink - - isn't it - -
brother Pedrillo?

PEDRILLO
Right, brother Osmin, right!

OSMIN
It makes one so lively
(he begins to nod)
- - so gay - - so merry.
Haven't you any more, brother?
*(He reaches for the second bottle,
which Pedrillo hands him)*

PEDRILLO
Look here, old man, don't drink
too much: it goes to your head.

OSMIN
Don't you worry; I'm as - -
sober as can be. But it's true - -
*(he begins to sway back and
forth on the ground)*
it tastes - - delicious!

PEDRILLO
(Nun wird's Zeit, ihn fortzuschaffen!)
Nun komm, Alter, komm, wir wollen
schlafen gehn!
(Er hebt ih auf)

OSMIN
Schlafen? Schämst du dich nicht?
Gift und Dolch! Wer wird denn so
schläfrig sein? - - es ist ja kaum Morgen - -

PEDRILLO
Ho, ho, die Sonne ist schon hinunter!
Komm, komm, dass uns der Bassa
nicht überrascht!

OSMIN
(im Abführen)
Ja, ja - - guter Bassa - - gute Nacht,
Brüderchen - - gute Nacht.
*(Pedrillo führt ihn hinein, kommt
aber gleich wieder zurück)*

PEDRILLO
(macht's Osmin nach)
Gute Nacht, Brüderchen - - gute Nacht!
Ach, kommen Sie, kommen Sie, liebster
Herr! Unser Argus ist blind, ich hab ihn
tüchtig zugedeckt.

BELMONTE
(kommt von links hinten)
O dass wir glücklich wären! Aber sag:
ist Konstanze noch nicht hier?

PEDRILLO
Eben kommt sie da den Gang herauf.
*(Konstanze und Blonde eilen von rechts
vorn herbei)*

KONSTANZE
O mein Belmonte!

BELMONTE
Ist's möglich?
(einander im Arm)

15.   ARIE

PEDRILLO
(Now's the time to get rid of him!)
Come now, old chap, let's go to
sleep!
(He helps him up)

OSMIN
Sleep? Aren't you ashamed? Fire
and fury, who wants to sleep?
It's not even morning yet - -

PEDRILLO
Ho, ho, the sun's already set.
Come on now, so's the Pasha
won't catch us!

OSMIN
(as he is led away)
Yes, yes - - good Pasha - - good night,
dear brother - - good night.
*(Pedrillo leads him away, but
returns immediately)*

PEDRILLO
(imitating Osmin)
Good night, dear brother - -
good night! Ah, come along, dear
master! Our Argus is blind; I've
just tucked him up cosily.

BELMONTE
(coming forward from the left)
I hope we're lucky. But tell me,
isn't Constanze here yet?

PEDRILLO
She's just coming along the path.
*(Constanze and Blonde hurry in
from the right)*

CONSTANZE
O my Belmonte!

BELMONTE
Is it possible?
(they embrace)

15.   ARIA

BELMONTE
Wenn der Freude Tränen fliessen,
lächelt Liebe dem Geliebten hold;
von den Wangen sie zu küssen
ist der Liebe schönster, grösster Sold.
Ach Konstanze, dich zu sehen,
dich voll Wonne, voll Entzücken
an dies treue Herz zu drücken,
lohnet mir nicht Kron' und Pracht.
Ha! Dieses sel'ge Wiederfinden,
lässt innig erst mich ganz empfinden
welchen Schmerz die Trennung macht.

BELMONTE
(spricht)
Ich hab hier ein Schiff in Bereitschaft.
Um Mitternacht, wenn alles schläft,
komm ich an dein Fenster, und dann
sei die Liebe unser Schutzengel!

16. QUARTETT

KONSTANZE
Ach, Belmonte, ach mein Leben!

BELMONTE
Ach, Konstanze, ach mein Leben!

KONSTANZE
Ist es möglich? Welch Entzücken!
Dich an meine Brust zu drücken
nach so vieler Tage Leid.

BELMONTE
Welche Wonne, dich zu finden!
Nun muss aller Kummer schwinden.
O, wie ist mein Herz erfreut!

KONSTANZE
Sieh, die Freudentränen fliessen.

BELMONTE
Holde, lass hinweg sie küssen!

KONSTANZE
Dass es doch die letzte sei!

BELMONTE
Ja, noch heute wirst du frei!

BELMONTE
When tears of joy are flowing,
love smiles on lovers:
to kiss their cheeks
is love's greatest, happiest reward.
Ah Constanze, to see you
and in rapture and bliss
to press you to my faithful heart
is a prize no royal crown could
match. Ah, to rediscover this bliss
I had first to experience to the full
all the pain of separation.

BELMONTE
(spoken)
I have a ship here in readiness.
At midnight, when all are asleep,
I'll come to your window, and
then let love be our guardian angel!

16. QUARTET

CONSTANZE
Ah Belmonte, my life!

BELMONTE
Ah Constanze, my life!

CONSTANZE
Is it possible? What enchantment
to clasp you to my breast
after so many days of suffering!

BELMONTE
What bliss to find you!
Now all grief must vanish.
O how my heart rejoices!

CONSTANZE
See, tears of joy are flowing.

BELMONTE
My fair one, let me kiss them away!

CONSTANZE
May they be our last tears!

BELMONTE
Yes, this very day you shall be free!

PEDRILLO
Also, Blondchen, hast's verstanden?
Alles ist zur Flucht vorhanden.
Um Schlag zwölfe sind wir da.

PEDRILLO
So, Blonde, do you understand?
Everything's ready for flight.
On the stroke of twelve we'll be there.

BLONDE
Unbesorgt, es wird nichts fehlen.
Die Minuten werd' ich zählen.
Wär' der Augenblick schon da!

BLONDE
Don't worry, nothing will go wrong.
I'll be counting the minutes.
If only the moment had already
come!

ALLE VIER
Endlich scheint die Hoffnungssonne
hell durchs trübe Firmament!
Voll Entzücken, Freud und Wonne
sehn wir unsrer Leiden End'!

ALL FOUR
At last the sun of hope is shining
brightly through the gloomy sky.
Filled with rapture, joy and bliss,
may we see the end of our suffering!

BELMONTE
Doch ach, bei aller Lust
empfindet meine Brust
noch manch geheime Sorgen!

BELMONTE
But yet, along with my joy,
my heart still feels
many a secret care!

KONSTANZE
Was ist es, Liebster, sprich!
Geschwind, erkläre dich!
O halt mir nichts verborgen!

CONSTANZE
What is it, dearest, say!
Quick, explain yourself!
Keep nothing back from me.

BELMONTE
Man sagt - - du seist - -

BELMONTE
It's said - - you are - -

KONSTANZE
Nun weiter?

CONSTANZE
Go on!

*(Sie sehen einander still schweigend
und furchtsam an)*

*(They look at each other mutely
and nervously)*

PEDRILLO
Doch Blondchen, ach, die Leiter!
Bist du wohl soviel wert?
(zeigt, dass er wage gehenkt zu werden)

PEDRILLO
But Blonde, the ladder!
Are you worth that much?
(indicates that he risks being hanged)

BLONDE
Hans Narr, schnappt's bei dir über?
Ei, hättest du nur lieber
die Frage umgekehrt.

BLONDE
Blockhead, have you gone daft?
You'd do better
to turn the question round.

PEDRILLO
Doch Herr Osmin . . .

PEDRILLO
But Osmin . . .

BLONDE
Lass hören!

BLONDE
Out with it!

144

KONSTANZE
Willst du dich nicht erklären?

CONSTANZE
Will you not explain?

BELMONTE
Ich will. Doch zürne nicht,
wenn ich nach dem Gerücht,
so ich gehört, es wage,
dich zitternd, bebend frage,
ob du den Bassa liebst?

BELMONTE
I will. But don't be angry
if, after the rumours
that I've heard, I dare
to ask you, quaking and trembling,
whether you love the Pasha?

PEDRILLO
Hat nicht Osmin fürwahr,
wie man fast glauben kann,
sein Recht als Herr probieret
und bei dir exerzieret?

PEDRILLO
Hasn't Osmin in fact,
as might well be believed,
tested his rights as your master
and exercised them on you?

KONSTANZE
O wie du mich betrübst!
(Sie weint)

CONSTANZE
O how you wound me!
(She weeps)

PEDRILLO
Dann wär's ein schlechter Kauf!

PEDRILLO
That'd be a bad bargain!

BLONDE
(gibt ihm eine Ohrfeige)
Da, nimm die Antwort drauf!

BLONDE
(boxing his ears)
There's your answer!

PEDRILLO
(hält sich die Backe)
Nun bin ich aufgeklärt.

PEDRILLO
(Holding his cheek)
Now I know.

BELMONTE
(knieend)
Konstanze, ach vergib!

BELMONTE
(kneeling)
Constanze, forgive me!

BLONDE
(zornig zu Pedrillo)
Du bist mich gar nicht wert!

BLONDE
(angrily to Pedrillo)
You're unworthy of me!

KONSTANZE
(seufzend, sich von Belmonte
wegwendend)
Ob ich dir treu verblieb?

CONSTANZE
(sighing, turning away from
Belmonte)
You ask if I've been true to you?

BLONDE
(zu Konstanze)
Der Schlingel fragt sich an,
ob ich ihm treu geblieben?

BLONDE
(to Constanze)
The knave asks
if I've been true to him?

KONSTANZE
(zu Blonde)
Dem Belmonte sagte man,
ich sollt' den Bassa lieben.

PEDRILLO
Dass Blonde ehrlich sei,
schwör ich bei allen Teufeln.

BELMONTE
Konstanze ist mir treu,
daran ist nicht zu zweifeln.

KONSTANZE & BLONDE
Wenn unsrer Ehre wegen
die Männer Argwohn hegen,
verdächtig auf uns sehn,
das ist nicht auszustehn!

BELMONTE & PEDRILLO
Sobald sich Weiber kränken,
wenn wir sie untreu denken,
dann sind sie wahrhaft treu,
von allem Vorwurf frei!

PEDRILLO
Liebstes Blondchen, ach, verzeihe!
Sieh, ich bau auf deine Treue
mehr jetzt als auf meinem Kopf!

BLONDE
Nein!

BELMONTE
Ach, Konstanze!

BLONDE
Das kann ich dir nicht schenken, nein,
mich mit so was zu verdenken,
mit dem alten, dummen Tropf!

BELMONTE
Ach, Konstanze, ach, mein Leben!
Könntest du mir doch vergeben,
dass ich diese Frage tat?

KONSTANZE
Belmonte, wie? Du könntest glauben,
das man dir dies Herz könnt' rauben,
das nur dir geschlagen hat?

CONSTANZE
(to Blonde)
Someone told Belmonte
that I'd given the Pasha my love.

PEDRILLO
That Blonde is faithful
I'd swear by all the devils.

BELMONTE
Constanze is true to me,
of that there is no doubt.

CONSTANZE & BLONDE
If men harbour doubts
about our honour
and regard us with suspicion,
this is not to be borne!

BELMONTE & PEDRILLO
As soon as women fret
if we think them unfaithful,
then they are really true
and free from all reproach!

PEDRILLO
Dearest Blonde, do forgive me!
See, now I put my faith more on
your fidelity than on my head!

BLONDE
No!

BELMONTE
Ah, Constanze!

BLONDE
I can't forgive you, no,
for thinking me capable of that,
and with that stupid old idiot!

BELMONTE
Ah Constanze, my life!
Can you ever forgive me
for asking that question?

CONSTANZE
What, Belmonte? Could you believe
that anyone could steal from you
this heart, which beats for you
alone?

PEDRILLO & BELMONTE
Ach verzeihe! Ich bereue!

KONSTANZE & BLONDE
Ich verzeihe deiner Reue!

ALLE VIER
Wohl, es sei nun abgetan!
Es lebe die Liebe!
Nur sie sei uns teuer,
nichts fache das Feuer
der Eifersucht an!

PEDRILLO & BELMONTE
Ah, forgive me! I'm sorry!

CONSTANZE & BLONDE
If you're sorry, I'll forgive you.

ALL FOUR
Good! Let that be an end to it!
Long live love!
Let it alone be held dear,
and let nothing fan
the flame of jealousy!

Dritte Aufzug

Act three

DRITTE AUFZUG

ACT THREE

Platz vor dem Palast des Bassa Selim. Auf der rechten Seite der Palast; gegenüber die Wohnung des Osmin; im Hintergrunde das Meer. Es ist Mitternacht.
Belmonte, Pedrillo

Square in front of the Pasha Selim's palace. On the right, the palace; opposite, Osmin's dwelling; in the background the sea. It is midnight.
Belmonte, Pedrillo

(gesprochen)

(spoken)

BELMONTE
(ruft leise)
Pedrillo! Pedrillo!

BELMONTE
(calling softly)
Pedrillo! Pedrillo!

PEDRILLO
Wie gerufen!

PEDRILLO
Present!

BELMONTE
Ist alles fertig gemacht?

BELMONTE
Is everything ready?

PEDRILLO
Alles! Jetzt will ich ein wenig um den Palast herum spionieren, wie's aussieht.

PEDRILLO
Everything! I'll just take a quick look round the palace and see what's what.

BELMONTE
Komm bald wieder.
(Pedrillo geht ab)
O Konstanze, wie schlägt mir das Herz!
O Liebe, sei du meine Leiterin!

BELMONTE
Come back quickly.
(Exit Pedrillo)
O Constanze, how my heart is throbbing! Love, be my guide!

17.   ARIE

17.   ARIA

BELMONTE
Ich baue ganz auf deine Stärke,
vertrau', o Liebe, deiner Macht;
denn ach! Was wurden nicht fur Werke
schon oft durch dich zu Stand' gebracht!
Was aller Welt unmöglich scheint,
wird durch die Liebe doch vereint.

(gesprochen)

PEDRILLO
(kommt herein)
Alles liegt auf dem Ohr. Es ist alles so
ruhig, so stille als den Tag nach der
Sündflut.

BELMONTE
Nun, lass uns sie befreien.
Wo ist die Leiter?

PEDRILLO
Nicht so hitzig. Ich muss erst das
Signal geben.

BELMONTE
Was hindert dich denn, es nicht zu tun?

PEDRILLO
Gehen Sie dort an die Ecke, und geben
Sie wohl acht, dass wir nicht überrascht
werden.

BELMONTE
Zaudre nur nicht!

(geht ab)

PEDRILLO
(indem er seine Mandoline her vorholt)
Nun, so sei es denn gewagt!

18. ROMANZE

PEDRILLO
*(singt zu Konstanzes Fenster hin und
akkompagniert sich)*
In Mohrenland gefangen war
ein Mädchen hübsch und fein;
sah rot und weiss, was schwarz
von Haar,
seufzt' Tag und Nacht und weinte gar,

BELMONTE
I build on your power,
o love; grant me your strength.
But ah! What deeds cannot be done
through your might! What seems
impossible to all the world
can be accomplished through love.

(spoken)

PEDRILLO
(entering)
Everyone's asleep. It's all as quiet
and still as the day after the
Great Flood.

BELMONTE
Well, let's rescue them.
Where's the ladder?

PEDRILLO
Not so fast. I've got to give the
signal first.

BELMONTE
Well, what's keeping you?

PEDRILLO
Go over to the corner and keep
a sharp lookout so that we won't
be surprised.

BELMONTE
Get on with it!

(exit)

PEDRILLO
(taking out his mandoline)
Well, here goes!

18. ROMANCE

PEDRILLO
*(singing to Constanze's window
and accompanying himself)*
In a Moorish land
a lovely maid was imprisoned;
pink and white was she, her hair
was black,
she sighed night and day

wollt' gern erlösen sein.
Da kam aus fremdem Land daher
ein tapf'rer Rittersmann,
den jammerte das Mädchen sehr.
"Ach!" rief er, "wag ich Kopf und Ehr
wenn ich sie retten kann".

(gesprochen)
Noch geht alles gut, es rührt sich
noch nichts.

BELMONTE
(kommt hervor)
Mach ein Ende, Pedrillo.

PEDRILLO
An mir liegt es nicht, dass sie sich noch
nicht zeigen. Entweder schlafen sie
fester als jemals, oder der Bassa is bei
der Hand. Wir wollen's weiter versuchen.
Bleiben Sie nur auf Ihrem Posten.

(Belmonte geht wieder fort)

PEDRILLO
(singt)
"Ich komm zu dir in finstrer Nacht,
Lass Liebchen, husch mich ein!
Ich fürchte weder Schloss noch Wacht.
Holla! Horch auf! Um Mitternacht
sollst du erlöset sein".
Gesagt, getan: Glock' zwölfe stand
der tapf're Ritter da;
sanft reicht' sie ihm die weiche Hand,
früh man die leere Zelle fand;
fort war sie, hopsasa!

KONSTANZE
(oben am Fenster)
Belmonte!

BELMONTE
Konstanze, hier bin ich.
Hurtig, die Leiter!

*(Pedrillo stellt die Leiter an Konstanzes
Fenster, Belmonte steigt hinein;
Pedrillo hält die Leiter)*

and wept bitterly,
longing to be rescued.
From a foreign land
there came a daring knight,
who grieved for the maid and cried
"I'll risk my head and my honour
to rescue her".
(spoken)
Nothing wrong so far:
everything's quiet.

BELMONTE
(coming out)
Have done, Pedrillo.

PEDRILLO
It's not my fault that they haven't
appeared yet. Either they're sleeping
more soundly than ever, or the
Pasha is around. Let's try again.
Please stay at your post.

(Belmonte goes off again)

PEDRILLO
(sings)
"I'll come to you at dead of night:
let me in quickly, dearest!
I fear neither lock nor guard.
Holla there! Listen! At midnight
you shall be freed".
He kept his word: at the stroke of
twelve the bold knight was there;
she gently gave him her soft hand;
in the early hours her cell was
found empty; she was off and away.

CONSTANZE
(above, at the window)
Belmonte!

BELMONTE
Constanze, here I am. The ladder,
quick!

*(Pedrillo places the ladder at
Constanze's window: Belmonte
climbs up while Pedrillo holds it)*

150

PEDRILLO
Je nu, der Anfang ist einmal gemacht,
jetzt ist's nicht mehr aufzuhalten. Es geht
nun schon einmal auf Leben oder auf
den Tod los!

BELMONTE
*(kommt mit Konstanze unten zur
Tür heraus)*
Nun, holder Engel, nun hab ich
dich wieder! Nichts soll uns mehr
trennen.

PEDRILLO
Nur fort, nicht geplaudert,
sonst könnt es freilich schief
gehen, wenn wir da lange
Rat halten und seufzen!
(stösst Belmonte und Konstanze fort)
Nur frisch nach dem Strande zu!
Ich komme gleich nach.

(Belmonte und Konstanze ab)

PEDRILLO
Nun, Kupido, halte mir dei Leiter und
hülle mich samt meine Gerätschaft in
einen dicken Nebel ein!

*(Er hat die Leiter an Blondes Fenster
gelegt und ist hinaufgestiegen)*
Blondchen, Blonchen, mach auf, um
Himmels willen, zaudre nicht! Es ist
um Hals und Kragen zu tun!
*(Er wird das Fenster geöffnet und
steigt hinein)*

*(Osmin und ein schwarzer Stummer
öffnen die Tür von Osmins Haus, wo
Pedrillo hineingestiegen ist. Osmin, noch
halb schlaftrunken, hat eine Laterne)*

OSMIN
Lärmen hörtest du? Was kann's denn
geben? . . . Gift und Dolch! Was ist
das? Wer kann ins Haus steigen?
Das sind Diebe oder Mörder. Hurtig,
hole die Wache! Ich will unterdessen
lauern.

PEDRILLO
Well, we've made a start, and now
there's no more turning back.
From here on it's life
or death.

BELMONTE
*(coming out of the door with
Constanze)*
Now, my sweet angel, you're
mine again! Nothing shall ever
part us any more.

PEDRILLO
Let's go; this is no time for chatter.
Everything can still go wrong if we
stand here making speeches and
sighing.
(pushes Belmonte and Constanze out)
Now quickly to the shore!
I'll be close behind you.

(Exeunt Belmonte and Constanze)

PEDRILLO
Now Cupid, hold the ladder and
conceal what I'm up to in a nice
thick cloud!

*(He has leaned the ladder against
Blonde's window and is climbing it)*
Blonde, Blonde, open up quickly,
for heaven's sake! My neck's at
stake!
*(The window is opened and he
steps inside)*

*(Osmin and a black mute open the
door of Osmin's house, into which
Pedrillo has climbed. Osmin, still
half dazed with sleep, has a lantern)*

OSMIN
You heard a noise? What could it be
be? . . . Fire and fury! What's that?
Who's climbing into my house?
It's either thieves or murderers.
Quick, call out the guards! I'll
keep watch meanwhile.

*(Der Stumme ab; Osmin setzt sich
auf die Leiter, mit der Laterne in
der Hand, und nickt ein. Pedrillo
kommt rückwärts wieder zum
Fenster herausgestiegen und will
die Leiter wieder herunter.)*

BLONDE
*(oben am Fenster, wird Osmin gewahr
und ruft Pedrillo zu)*
O Himmel, Pedrillo, wir sind verloren!

PEDRILLO
*(sieht sich um, und sowie er Osmin gewahr
wird, stuzt er, besieht ihn und steigt
wieder zum Fenster hinein)*
Ach, welcher Teufel hat sich wider uns
verschworen!

OSMIN
Wart, spitzbube, du sollst mir nicht
entkommen. Hilfe, hilfe! Wache! Hurtig,
hier gibt's Räuber! Herbei, herbei!
*(Pedrillo kommt mit Blonde unten zur
Haustür heraus, sieht schüchtern nach
der Leiter und schleicht sich dann mit
Blonde darunter weg)*

WACHE
*(mit Fackeln, halten Osmin auf,
der will nach)*
Halt, halt! Wohin?
Wer bist du?

OSMIN
Nur nicht lange gefragt, sonst entkommen
die Spitzbuben. Seht ihr denn nicht? Hier
ist noch die Leiter.
*(Ein Teil der Wache bringt Pedrillo
und Blonde zurück)*
Ach endlich! Gift und Dolch! Seh ich
recht? Ihr beide? Warte, spitzbübischer
Pedrillo, dein Kopf soll am längsten
festgestanden sein.

*(Exit the mute. Osmin sits on the
ladder, the lantern in his hand, and
nods off. Pedrillo comes out of
the window backwards and is
about to start down the ladder
again.*

BLONDE
*(at the window, perceives Osmin and
calls to Pedrillo)*
O heavens! Pedrillo, we're lost!

PEDRILLO
*(looks round, and seeing Osmin
stops short and climbs back
through the window)*
O, what evil spirit is conspiring
against us?

OSMIN
Wait, rascal, you shan't escape!
Help, help! Guards! Quick, robbers!
Here, over here!
*(Pedrillo comes out of the door with
Blonde, looks round furtively at the
ladder and then slips off with
Blonde)*

GUARDS
*(with torches, restraining Osmin,
who is trying to follow them)*
Halt! Where are you going?
Who are you?

OSMIN
Don't keep asking questions or the
rascals will get away. Can't you see
them? Here's the ladder still.
*(Some of the guards bring back
Pedrillo and Blonde).*
Ah, at last! Fire and fury, do I see
aright? You two? Just wait,
Pedrillo you scoundrel, your head
shall finally answer for this.

PEDRILLO
Brüderchen, wirst doch Spass verstehn?
Ich wollt' dir dein Weibchen nur ein
wenig spazieren führen, weil du heute
dazu nicht aufgelegt bist. Du weisst schon
(heimlich zu Osmin),
wegen des Cyperweins.

PEDRILLO
Dear brother, can't you take a
joke? I wanted to take your wife
for a little walk, because you
weren't up to it today. You know
(privately to Osmin),
because of the Cyprus wine.

OSMIN
Schurke, hier verstehe ich keinen Spass;
dein Kopf muss herunter, so wahr ich
ein Muselmann bin.

OSMIN
Scoundrel! I see nothing funny in
this: your head shall roll, as true as
I'm a Moslem.

*(Ein anderer Teil der Wache, auch
mit Fackeln, bringt Belmonte und
Konstanze)*

*(Other guards, also with torches,
bring in Belmonte and
Constanze)*

BELMONTE
(wiedersetzt sich noch)
Schändliche, lasst mich los! Hier ist ein
Beutel mit Zechinen; er ist euer, und
noch zweimal so viel: lasst mich los.

BELMONTE
(still struggling)
Wretches, let me go. Here's a purse
of money: it's yours, and twice as
much, if you let me go.

KONSTANZE
Lasst euch bewegen!

CONSTANZE
Have pity on us!

OSMIN
Euer Geld brauchen wir nicht, das
bekommen wir ohnehin! Eure Kopfe
wollen wir.
(zur Wache)
Schleppt sie fort zum Bassa!

OSMIN
We don't need your money: we'll
get it anyway. It's your heads we
want.
(to the guards)
Take them off to the Pasha!

BELMONTE & KONSTANZE
Habt doch Erbarmen! Lasst Euch
bewegen!

BELMONTE & CONSTANZE
Have mercy!
Pity us!

OSMIN
Um nichts in der Welt! Ich habe mir
längst so einen Augenblick gewünscht.
Fort, fort!

OSMIN
Not for anything in the world!
I've waited a long time for this.
Away with them!

*(Die Wache führt Belmonte und
Konstanze fort, samt Pedrillo und
Blonde)*

*(The guards lead off Belmonte
and Constanze, along with
Pedrillo and Blonde)*

19. ARIE

19. ARIA

OSMIN
O wie will ich triumphieren,
wenn sie euch zum Richtplatz führen
und die Hälse schnüren zu!
Hupfen will ich, lachen, springen
und ein Freudenliedchen singen.
Denn nun hab ich vor euch Ruh.
Schleicht nur säuberlich und leise,
ihr verdammten Haremsmäuse,
unser Ohr entdeckt euch schon.
Und eh' ihr uns könnt entspringen,
seht ihr euch in unsern Schlingen
und erhaschet euren Lohn.

OSMIN
O how I shall triumph
when they lead you to the gallows
and string you up by the neck!
I shall gambol, laugh and skip
and croon a little song of joy,
for then I shall be rid of you.
However softly and cautiously
you creep, you damned harem-mice,
our ears soon detect you,
and before you can escape us
you find yourselves in our trap
and receive your just deserts.

VERWANDLUNG

CHANGE OF SCENE

Zimmer des Bassa.
Selim, Osmin.

The Pasha's apartment.
Selim, Osmin.

(gesprochen)

(spoken)

OSMIN
Herr, verzeih, dass ich es so früh wage,
deine Ruhe zu stören! Herr, es ist die
schändlichste Verräterei in deinem
Palast . . .

OSMIN
Master, forgive me for daring to
disturb your sleep so early.
Master, the most shameful
treachery in your palace . . .

SELIM
Verräterei?

SELIM
Treachery?

OSMIN
Die niederträchtigen Christensklaven
entführen uns die Weiber. Der grosse
Baumeister, den du gestern auf Zureden
des Verräters Pedrillo aufnahmst, hat
deine schöne Konstanze entführt.
Meiner Wachsamkeit hast du es zu
danken, dass ich sie wieder beim Schopf
gekriegt habe. Auch mir selbst hatte
der spitzbübische Pedrillo eine gleiche
Ehre zugedacht, und er hatte mein
Blondchen schon beim Kopf.

OSMIN
The base Christian slaves are
stealing our women from us. The
great architect you engaged
yesterday on the advice of the
traitor Pedrillo has stolen your
lovely Constanze. But thanks to
my watchfulness, I've caught
them again. And that thief
Pedrillo paid me a similar
honour: he'd gone off
with my little Blonde.

*(Belmonte und Konstanza werden von
der Wache hereingeführt)*

*(Belmonte and Constanze are
brought in by the guards)*

154

SELIM
Ah, Verräter! Ist's möglich? Ha, du
heuchlerische Sirene! War das der
Aufschub, den du begehrtest?
Missbrauchtest du so die Nachsicht,
die ich dir gab, um mich zu hintergehen?

KONSTANZE
Ich bin strafbar in deinen Augen,
Herr, es ist wahr; aber es ist mein
Geliebter, mein einziger Geliebter,
dem lang schon dieses Herz gehört.
O lass mich sterben! Gern, gern will
ich den Tod erdulden, aber schone
nur sein Leben . . .

SELIM
Und du wagst's, Unverschämte, für ihn
zu bitten?

KONSTANZE
Noch mehr: für ihn zu sterben!

BELMONTE
Ha, Bassa! Noch nie erniedrigte ich mich
zu bitten, noch nie hat dieses Knie sich
vor einem Menschen gebeugt: aber sieh,
hier lieg ich zu deinen Füssen und flehe
dein Mitleid an. Ich bin vor einer
grossen spanischen Familie, man wird
alles für mich zahlen. Lass dich bewegen,
bestimme sein Lösegeld für mich und
Konstanze so hoch du willst. Mein Name
ist Lostados.

SELIM
(staunend)
Was hor' ich? Der Kommandant von
Oran, ist er dir bekannt?

BELMONTE
Das is mein Vater.

SELIM
Dein Vater? Welcher glückliche Tag,
den Sohn meines ärgsten Feindes in
meiner Macht zu haben! Kann was
angenehmeres sein? Wisse, Elender,
dein Vater, dieser Barbar, ist schuld,
dass ich mein Vaterland verlassen musste.

SELIM
Ah, traitor! Is it possible? And you
deceitful siren! Was that why you
asked for a delay? Is this how you
abuse the trust I gave you, to
betray me?

CONSTANZE
In your eyes I am guilty, my
lord, it is true; but it is my beloved,
my only beloved here, to whom my
heart has long been given.
O let me die! Gladly, gladly will
I suffer death, only spare his
life . . .

SELIM
You dare, shameless one, to
plead for him?

CONSTANZE
Still more - - to die for him!

BELMONTE
Pasha! Never before have I
lowered myself to beg; never
before has this knee bent to any
man. But now I lie at your feet
and implore your mercy. I am of
a great Spanish family, who will
pay whatever you ask. Have mercy!
Set as high a ransom for myself
and Constanze as you wish. My
name is Lostados.

SELIM
(amazed)
What can I hear? Do you know the
commandant of Oran?

BELMONTE
He is my father.

SELIM
Your father? What a lucky day,
to have the son of my arch-enemy
in my power! Could anything be
more delightful? Know, wretch,
that your father, that barbarian,
is responsible for my having to

Sein unbiegsamer Geiz entriss mir
eine Geliebte, die ich höher als mein
Leben schätzte. Er brachte mich um
Ehrenstellen, Vermögen, um alles.
Kurz, er zernichtete mein ganzes
Glück. Wie er mit mir verfahren ist,
will ich mit dir verfahren. Folge
mir, Osmin, ich will dir Befehle
zu ihren Martern geben.
(zu der Wache)
Bewacht sie hier.

(Er geht ab, Osmin folgt)

20. REZITATIV UND DUETT

BELMONTE
Welch ein Geschick! O Qual der Seele!
Hat sich denn alles wider mich verschworen?
Ach, Konstanze, durch mich bist du
verloren!
Welch eine Pein!

KONSTANZE
Lass, ach Geliebter, lass dich das nicht
quälen.
Was ist der Tod? Ein Übergang zur Ruh!
Und dann, an deiner Seite
ist er Vorgeschmack der Seligkeit.

BELMONTE
Engelsseele! Welch holde Güte!
Du flösset Trost in mein erschuttert Herz,
du linderst mir den Todesschmerz,
und ach, ich reisse dich ins Grab!
Ha, du solltest für mich sterben!
Ach, Konstanze, kann ich's wagen,
noch die Augen aufzuschlagen?
Ich bereite dir den Tod!

KONSTANZE
Belmont, du stirbst meinetwegen,
ich nur zog dich ins Verderben,
und ich soll nicht mit dir sterben?
Wonne ist mir dies Gebot!

BEIDE
Ach Geliebte(r)! Dich zu lieben
war mein Wunsch und all mein Streben!
Ohne dich ist mir's nur Pein,
länger auf der Welt zu sein.

leave my native land. His insatiable
greed deprived me of my beloved,
whom I cherished more than my life.
He robbed me of honours, property,
everything: in brief, he destroyed
my whole happiness. As he dealt
with me, so I shall deal with you.
Follow me, Osmin I will give you
instructions for their torture.
(to the guards)
Watch them well!

(Exit, followed by Osmin)

20. RECITATIVE AND DUET

BELMONTE
What a fate! O torment of the soul!
Has everything conspired against
me? Ah, Constanze, through me you
are lost! What grief!

CONSTANZE
Ah beloved, let that not torment
you. What is death? A passage to
peace! And then, at your side,
a foretaste of bliss.

BELMONTE
Angelic soul! How gentle and good
you are! You pour balm into my
anguished heart, you soften for
me the pain of death, and I, alas,
drag you to the grave! Alas, you
are to die for me! Ah Constanze,
how can I dare still to look you
in the eyes? I have brought about
your death!

CONSTANZE
Belmonte, you are to die on my
account, I alone brought you to
destruction, and may I not die
with you? This command brings
me bliss!

BOTH
Ah beloved! To love you was
all I wished and strove for!
Without you it is only pain for
me to stay longer in this world.

BELMONTE
Ich will alles gerne leiden,

KONSTANZE
Ruhig sterb ich und mit Freuden,

BEIDE
weil ich dir zur Seite bin.
Für dich, Geliebte(r),
geb ich gern Mein Leben hin!
O welche Seligkeit!
Mit der (dem) Geliebten zu sterben
ist seliges Entzücken!
Mit wonnevollen Blicken
verlässt man da die Welt!

*(Pedrillo und Blonde werden von einem
andern Teil der Wache hereingeführt)*

(gesprochen)

PEDRILLO
(zu Belmonte)
Ach, Herr, wir sind hin! An Rettung ist
nicht mehr zu denken. Ach, Blondchen,
Blondchen, was werden sie wohl mit
dir anfangen?

BLONDE
Das gilt mir nun ganz gleich. Da es einmal
gestorben sein muss, ist mir alles recht.

(Selim und Osmin treten ein)

SELIM
Nun, Sklave! Elender Sklave!
Erwartest du dein Urteil?

BELMONTE
Ja, Bassa, mit so vieler Kaltblütigkeit,
als hitze du es aussprechen kannst. Kühle
deine Rache an mir, tilge das Unrecht,
so mein Vater dir angetan! Ich
erwarte alles und tadle dich
nicht.

SELIM
Du betrügst dich. Ich habe deinen Vater
viel zu sehr verabscheut, als dass ich je
in seine Fusstapfen treten könnte. Nimm

BELMONTE
I will suffer anything gladly,

CONSTANZE
I will die peacefully and joyfully,

BOTH
since I am at your side.
For you, beloved,
I gladly give my life!
O what rapture!
To die with one's beloved
is rapture and bliss!
One then quits this world
in the joy of loving glances!

*(Pedrillo and Blonde are brought
in by another group of guards)*

(spoken)

PEDRILLO
(to Belmonte)
O master, we're back! Escape is
out of the question now. O poor
little Blonde! What will they do
to you.

BLONDE
It doesn't really matter. Since I
have to die it's all the same to me.

(Enter Selim and Osmin)

SELIM
Now, miserable slave!
Are you ready for your sentence?

BELMONTE
Yes, Pasha, I await it as calmly as
you speak heatedly. Cool your
wrath on me, cancel out the
wrong my father did you! I am
prepared for anything and do
not blame you.

SELIM
You are mistaken. I hold your
father in too much detestation to
be able to tread in his footsteps.

157

deine Freiheit, nimm Konstanze, segle
in dein Vaterland, sage deinem Vater, dass
du in meiner Gewalt warst, dass ich dich
freigelassen, um ihn sagen zu könne, es
wäre ein weit grösser Vernugen, eine
erlittene Ungerechtigkeit durch Wohltaten
zu vergelten, als Laster mit Lastern tilgen.

BELMONTE
Herr! Du setzest mich in Erstaunen . . .

SELIM
(ihn verächtlich ansehend)
Das glaub ich. Zieh damit hin,
und werde du wenigstens
menschlicher als dein Vater,
so ist meine Handlung belohnt.

KONSTANZE
Herr, vergib! Ich schätzte
bisher deine edle Seele, aber
nun bewundere ich . . .

PEDRILLO
(fällt ihm zu Füssen)
Herr, dürfen wir beide Unglückliche
es auch wagen, um Gnade zu flehen?
Ich war von Jugend auf ein treuer
Diener meines Herrn.

OSMIN
Beim Allah, lass dich ja nicht von dem
verwünschten Schmarotzer hintergehn!
Er hat schon hundertmal den Tod
verdient.

SELIM
Er mag ihn also in seinem Vaterlande
suchen.
(zur Wache)
Man begleite alle vier an das Schiff.

OSMIN
Wie, meine Blonde soll er auch
mitnehmen? Gift und Dolch!
Ich möchte bersten.

SELIM
Beruhige dich. Wen man durch Wohltun
nicht für sich gewinnen kann, den muss
man sich vom Halse schaffen.

Take your freedom, take Constanze,
sail home, and tell your father that
you were in my power and I set
you free so that you could tell him
that it is a far greater pleasure to
repay an injustice with a favour
than an evil with an evil.

BELMONTE
My lord! You astonish me . . .

SELIM
(looking at him with contempt)
I can believe that. Reflect on this,
and if you become at least more
humane than your father, my
action will be rewarded.

CONSTANZE
My lord, forgive me! Hitherto
I had esteemed your noble soul,
but now I marvel . . .

PEDRILLO
(falling at his feet)
Lord, dare we two unhappy beings
also crave your mercy?
Since childhood I've been a
faithful servant to my master.

OSMIN
By Allah! Don't let this cursed
sponger deceive you! He has
earned death a hundred times
over.

SELIM
Then let him find it in his
native land.
(to the guards)
Escort all four of them to the ship.

OSMIN
What, is he to take my little
Blonde with him too? Fire and
fury! I shall explode.

SELIM
Calm yourself. If you can't win
someone by kindness it is better
to give them up.

21. VAUDEVILLE

BELMONTE
Nie werd ich deine Huld verkennen;
mein Dank bleibt ewig dir geweiht,
an jedem Ort, zu jeder Zeit
werd ich dich gross und edel nennen.
Wer so viel Huld vergessen kann,
den seh' man mit Verachtung an.

**KONSTANZE, BLONDE, BELMONTE,
PEDRILLO, OSMIN**
Wer so viel Huld vergessen kann,
den seh' man mit Verachtung
an.

KONSTANZE
Nie werd ich, selbst im Schoss der Liebe,
vergessen, was der Dank gebeut;
mein Herz, der Liebe nun geweiht,
hegt auch dem Dank geweihte Triebe.
Wer so viel Huld vergessen kann,
den seh' man mit Verachtung an.

**KONSTANZE, BLONDE, BELMONTE,
PEDRILLO, OSMIN**
Wer so viel Huld vergessen kann,
den seh' man vit Verachtung an.

PEDRILLO
Wenn ich es je vergessen könnte,
wie nah' ich am Erdrosseln war,
und all der anderen Gefahr,
Ich lief' als ob der Kopf mir brennte.
Wer so viel Huld vergessen kann,
den seh' man vit Verachtung an.

**KONSTANZE, BLONDE, BELMONTE,
PEDRILLO, OSMIN**
Wer so viel Huld vergessen kann,
deh seh' man mit Verachtung an.

21. VAUDEVILLE

BELMONTE
Never shall I fail to appreciate your
mercy; I shall always owe you
gratitude; at all times and places
I shall call you great and noble.
Anyone who could forget so great
a favour should be looked on with
contempt.

**CONSTANZE, BLONDE, BELMONTE,
PEDRILLO, OSMIN**
Anyone who could forget so great
a favour should be looked on with
contempt.

CONSTANZE
Even in love's embrace, I shall never
forget the gratitude I owe;
my heart, now dedicated to love,
will also cherish grateful thanks.
Anyone who could forget so great
a favour should be looked on with
contempt.

**CONSTANZE, BLONDE, BELMONTE,
PEDRILLO, OSMIN**
Anyone who could forget so great
a favour should be looked on with
contempt.

PEDRILLO
If I could ever forget how near I
was to being throttled and all
the other dangers, I'd deserve
to have singing in my head.
Anyone who could forget so great
a favour should be looked on with
contempt.

**CONSTANZE, BLONDE, BELMONTE,
PEDRILLO, OSMIN**
Anyone who could forget so great
a favour should be looked on with
contempt.

BLONDE
Nehmt meinen Dank mit tausend Freuden,
Herr Bassa, lebt gesund und froh!
Osmin, das Schicksal will es so,
ich muss von dir auf ewig scheiden.
Wer so wie du nur zanken kann,
den seh' man vit Verachtung an!

BLONDE
Accept my thanks with a thousand-
fold joy, Pasha, health and
happiness to you! Osmin, fate has
willed it that I must leave you for
ever. Anyone who, like you, can
only quarrel should be looked
on with contempt.

OSMIN
Verbrennen sollte man die Hunde,
die uns so schändlich hintergehn.
Es ist nicht länger anzusehn.
Mir starrt die Zunge fast im Munde,
um ihren Lohn zu ordnen an:
erst geköpft, dann gehangen,
dann gespiesst auf heisse Stangen,
dann verbrannt, dann gebunden,
dann getaucht; zuletzt geschunden.

OSMIN
We should burn these dogs, who
have so disgracefully deceived us.
It's no longer to be borne.
My tongue goes almost rigid in
my mouth to order their reward:
first beheaded, then hanged,
then impaled on red-hot spikes,
then burned, then bound,
then submerged, finally flayed.

(läuft voll Wuth ab)

(rushes out in a rage)

KONSTANZE, BLONDE, BELMONTE, PEDRILLO
Nichts ist so hässlich als die Rache.
Grossmütig, menschlich, gütig sein
und ohne Eigennutz verzeihn,
ist nur der grossen Seelen Sache!

CONSTANZE, BLONDE, BELMONTE, PEDRILLO
Nothing is as hateful as revenge.
To be generous, merciful, kind
and selflessly to forgive
is the mark of a noble soul!

KONSTANZE
Wer dieses nicht erkennen kann,
den seh' man mit Verachtung an.

CONSTANZE
Anyone who could forget this
should be looked on with contempt.

KONSTANZE, BLONDE, BELMONTE, PEDRILLO
Wer dieses nicht erkennen kann
den seh' man vit Verachtung an.

CONSTANZE, BLONDE, BELMONTE, PEDRILLO
Anyone who could forget this
should be looked on with contempt.

(sie wenden sich zur Barke)

(they make their way towards the ship)

JANITSCHAREN
Bassa Selim lebe lange!
Ehre sei sein Eigentum!
Seine holde Scheitel prange
voll von Jubel, voll von Ruhm.
Bassa Selim lebe lange!

JANISSARIES
Long live the Pasha Selim!
Let honour be his!
May his noble brow be resplendent
with jubilation and fame.
Long live the Pasha Selim!

Discography

(All English disc numbers are given in roman type; *all USA numbers in italic type*)

DIE ZAUBERFLÖTE

Complete Sets

	SET A	SET B (no dialogue)
PAMINA	Lorengar	Janowitz
QUEEN OF THE NIGHT	Deutekom	Popp
TAMINO	Burrows	Gedda
SARASTRO	Talvela	Frick
PAPAGENO	Prey	Berry
SPEAKER	Fischer-Dieskau	Crass
PAPAGENA	Holm	Putz
LADIES	van Bork	Schwarzkopf
	Minton	Ludwig
	Plumacher	Hoffgen
Ensemble	Vienna Phil.	Philharmonia
Conductor	Solti	Klemperer
Disc Nos.	SET 479/81	SAN 137/9
		S 3651
Highlights		ASD 2314
		S 36315

	SET C	SET D
PAMINA	Lear	Güden
QUEEN OF THE NIGHT	Peters	Lipp
TAMINO	Wunderlich	Simoneau
SARASTRO	Crass	Böhme
PAPAGENO	Fischer-Dieskau	Berry
SPEAKER	Hotter	Schöffler
PAPAGENA	Otto	Loose
LADIES	Hillebrecht	Hollwig
	Ahlin	Ludwig
	Wagner	Rossl-Majdan
Ensemble	Berlin Phil.	Vienna Phil.
Conductor	Böhm	Böhm
Disc Nos.	2709017	GOS 501/3
	2709017	*Rich. 63507*
Highlights		SDD 218

Earlier versions

Lemnitz; Berger; Beilke; Roswänge; Strienz; Hüsch. Berlin, Beecham.
ALP 1273/5, *Turn. 4111/3.*

Seefried; Lipp; Jurinac; Loose; Dermota; Weber; Kunz. Vienna, Karajan.
CX1013/5

Greindl; Streich; Stader; Guillaume; Häfliger; Fischer-Dieskau; Borg; Klose.
Berlin, Fricsay. LPM 18267-9

Bijster; Tyler; Goren; Geschwend; Koekman. Dutch, Krannhals.
MMS 2033

Highlight only versions

Lipp; Schock; Frick; Kunz; Hallstein. Berlin, Hollreiser.
GERMANY 73739KR

Wunderlich; Gunther; Vivarelli; Roth-Ehrang; Giebel; Duske. Hamburg, Rother.
FRANCE Orphée 60027

Micheau; Robin; Linval; Monteil; Giraudeau; Dens; Depraz. *c* Froment (in French)
FRANCE PM 30509

DIE ENTFÜHRUNG AUS DEM SERAIL

Complete Sets

	SET A	SET B	SET C
CONSTANZE	Marshall	Rothenberger	Koth
BLONDE	Hollweg	Popp	Schädle
BELMONTE	Simoneau	Gedda	Wunderlich
PEDRILLO	Unger	Unger	Lenz
OSMIN	Frick	Frick	Böhme
Ensemble	Royal P.O.	Vienna Opera	Bavarian Opera
Conductor	Beecham	Krips	Jochum
Disc Nos.	HQS1050/1	SOC235/6	2709021
	S3555	*Ser S6025*	*2709021*

	SET D	SET E	SET F
CONSTANZE	Dobbs	Lipp	Stader
BLONDE	Eddy	Loose	Streich
BELMONTE	Gedda	Ludwig	Häfliger
PEDRILLO	Fryatt	Klein	Vantin
OSMIN	Mangin	Koreh	Greindl
Ensemble	Bath Festival	Vienna Opera	R.I.A.S.
Conductor	Menuhin	Krips	Fricsay
Disc Nos.	*(in English)*	LXT2536/8	18184/5
	SAN 201-3	*Rich 63015*	*18184/5*
	Ang S3741		

Also available in USA: *Turn. 34320/1* and GB: SFL14000/1
  w. Vulpius; Ronisch; Appreck; Forster; van Mill; Schutte. Dresden Opera, Suitner;
  also listed in USA on *Period TE1102* as performed by the Patagonia Festival
  Ch. & Orch.